LITTLE PUFFERS

A Guide to Britain's Narrow Gauge Railways 2015-2016

EDITOR
John Robinson

Eleventh Edition

RAILWAY LOCATOR MAP

The numbers shown on this map relate to the page numbers for each railway. Pages 5-6 contain an alphabetical listing of the railways featured in this guide. Please note that the markers on this map show the approximate location only.

ACKNOWLEDGEMENTS

We were greatly impressed by the friendly and cooperative manner of the staff and helpers of the railways which we selected to appear in this book, and wish to thank them all for the help they have given. In addition we wish to thank Bob Budd (cover design), Michael Robinson (page layouts) and Jonathan James (who provided a number of photographs) for their help.

Although we believe that the information contained in this guide is accurate at the time of going to press, we, and the Railways and Museums itemised, are unable to accept liability for any loss, damage, distress or injury suffered as a result of any inaccuracies. Furthermore, we and the Railways are unable to guarantee operating and opening times which may always be subject to cancellation without notice, particularly during adverse weather conditions.

If you feel we should include other locations or information in future editions, please let us know so that we may give them consideration. We would like to thank you for buying this guide and wish you 'Happy Railway Travelling'!

John Robinson

EDITOR

British Library Cataloguing in Publication Data
A catalogue record for this book is available from the British Library

ISBN-13:   978-1-86223-306-5

Copyright © 2015, MARKSMAN PUBLICATIONS. (01472 696226)
72 St. Peter's Avenue, Cleethorpes, N.E. Lincolnshire, DN35 8HU, England

The Publishers and respective Railways are unable to accept liability for any loss, damage or injury caused by error or inaccuracy in the information published in this guide.

Manufactured in the UK by Ashford Colour Press Ltd.

FOREWORD

For the purposes of this publication, we define railways solely by their gauge and include only those with a gauge in excess of 7¼ inches but less than UK Standard gauge. We also publish 'Still Steaming', a separate guide for Standard gauge railways and 'Tiny Trains', a guide for railways with gauges of 7¼ inches and smaller. Both of these guides, as well as further copies of 'Little Puffers' can be ordered UK post free from the Marksman Publications address opposite.

The cover photograph was provided by Jonathan James and shows the splendid locomotive 'Winston Churchill' in steam on the Romney, Hythe and Dymchurch Railway during 2014.

CONTENTS

Locator Map (North) 2
Locator Map (South) 3
Acknowledgments 4
Foreword and Contents 5-6
Abbey Pumping Station 7
Alford Valley Railway 8
Almond Valley Light Railway 9
Amberley Museum & Heritage Centre 10
Amerton Railway 11
Apedale Valley Light Railway 12
Astley Green Colliery Museum 13
Audley End Steam Railway 14
Bala Lake Railway 15
Bickington Steam Railway 16
Bicton Woodland Railway 17
Brecon Mountain Railway 18
Bredgar & Wormshill Light Railway 19
Bure Valley Railway 20
Cleethorpes Coast Light Railway 21
The Corris Railway 22
Derbyshire Dales Narrow Gauge Railway 23
Devon Railway Centre 24
Eastleigh Lakeside Railway 25
East Suffolk Light Railway 26
Evesham Vale Light Railway 27
Exbury Gardens Railway 28
Fairbourne Railway 29
Faversham Miniature Railway 30
Ferry Meadows Miniature Railway 31
Ffestiniog Railway 32
Gartell Light Railway 33
Giant's Causeway & Bushmills Railway 34
Golden Valley Light Railway 35
Great Laxey Mine Railway 36
Great Whipsnade Railway 37
Groudle Glen Railway 38
Hall Leys Miniature Railway 39
Hastings Miniature Railway 40
Hayling Seaside Railway 41

Heatherslaw Light Railway 42
Isle of Man Steam Railway 43
Kerr's Miniature Railway 44
Kirklees Light Railway 45
Lakeshore Railroad 46
Lappa Valley Steam Railway 47
Launceston Steam Railway 48
Leadhills & Wanlockhead Railway 49
Leeds Industrial Museum 50
Leighton Buzzard Railway 51
Lincolnshire Coast Light Railway 52
Littlehampton Railway 53
Llanberis Lake Railway 54
London Museum of Water & Steam 55
Lynton & Barnstaple Railway 56
Margam Park Railway 57
Moseley Industrial Narrow Gauge Tramway, Toy & Mining Museum 58
National Coal Mining Museum for England 59
Newby Hall Miniature Railway 60
North Bay Miniature Railway 61
Old Kiln Light Railway 62
Perrygrove Railway 63
Ravenglass & Eskdale Railway 64
Rhiw Valley Light Railway 65
Rhyl Miniature Railway 66
Romney, Hythe & Dymchurch Railway 67
Royal Victoria Railway 68
Rudyard Lake Steam Railway 69
Ruislip Lido Railway 70
Saltburn Miniature Railway 71
Sherwood Forest Railway 72
Sittingbourne & Kemsley Light Railway 73
Snowdon Mountain Railway 74
South Downs Light Railway 75
Southend Pier Railway 76
South Tynedale Railway 77
Steeple Grange Light Railway 78
Sutton Hall Railway 79
Talyllyn Railway 80
Teifi Valley Railway 81
Threlkeld Quarry Railway 82
Toddington Narrow Gauge Railway 83
Vale of Rheidol Railway 84
Volks Electric Railway 85
Watford Miniature Railway 86
Waveney Valley Railway 87
Wells Harbour Railway 88
Wells & Walsingham Light Railway 89
Welsh Highland Heritage Railway 90
Welsh Highland Railway (now part of the Ffestiniog Railway) 91
Welshpool & Llanfair Light Railway 92
West Lancashire Light Railway 93
Wicksteed Park Railway 94
Windmill Animal Farm Railway 95
Woodhorn Narrow Gauge Railway 96

ABBEY PUMPING STATION

Address: Abbey Pumping Station Museum, Corporation Road, Leicester, LE4 5PX	**Nº of Steam Locos**: 1
	Nº of Other Locos: 4
	Nº of Members: Approximately 140
Telephone Nº: (0116) 299-5113	**Annual Membership Fee**: £8.00 Adult
Year Formed: 1980s	**Approx Nº of Visitors P.A.**: 60,000
Location of Line: Leicester	**Gauge**: 2 feet
Length of Line: 300 yards	**Web site**: www.abbeypumpingstation.org

GENERAL INFORMATION

Nearest Mainline Station: Leicester London Road (3 miles)
Nearest Bus Station: Leicester (1½ miles)
Car Parking: Free parking available on site (Free parking at the Space Centre on Special Event days)
Coach Parking: Use the Space Centre car park
Souvenir Shop(s): Yes
Food & Drinks: Available on special event days only

SPECIAL INFORMATION

The Museum is situated in the Abbey Pumping Station which, from 1891 to 1964 pumped Leicester's sewage to nearby treatment works. The Museum now collects and displays the industrial, technological and scientific heritage of Leicester and contains rare working examples of Woolf compound rotative beam engines which are in steam on selected days.

OPERATING INFORMATION

Opening Times: The Pumping Station is open daily from February to October, 11.00am to 4.30pm. Trains run on the dates detailed below.
Steam Working: Selected Special Event days only: 2015 dates: 12th April; 2nd & 26th May; 6th & 27th June; 4th & 21st July; 1st & 18th August; 6th September; 3rd, 20th & 26th October; 7th & 28th November; 6th December; 10th January 2016; 7th February 2016.
Prices: Adults £3.50 (Special event days only)
Concessions £2.50 (Special events only)
Family £8.00 (Special event days only)

Detailed Directions by Car:
From All Parts: The Museum is situated next to the National Space Centre, about 1 mile North of Leicester city centre near Beaumont Leys and Belgrave. Brown tourist signs with a distinctive rocket logo provide directions to the NSC from the arterial routes around Leicester and the Museum is nearby.

ALFORD VALLEY RAILWAY

Address: Alford Station, Main Street, Alford, Aberdeenshire AB33 8HH	**Nº of Steam Locos**: None at present
Telephone Nº: 07879 293934	**Nº of Other Locos**: 3
Year Formed: 1979	**Approx Nº of Visitors P.A.**: 12,000
Location of Line: Alford – Haughton Park	**Gauge**: 2 feet
Length of Line: 1 mile	**Web site**: www.alfordvalleyrailway.org.uk
	E-mail: info@alfordvalleyrailway.org.uk

GENERAL INFORMATION

Nearest Mainline Station: Insch (10 miles)
Nearest Bus Station: Alford (200 yards)
Car Parking: Available on site
Coach Parking: Available on site
Souvenir Shop(s): Yes
Food & Drinks: The railway hopes to be able to provide refreshments during 2015.

SPECIAL INFORMATION

The Grampian Transport Museum is adjacent to the Railway and the Heritage Centre also has horse-drawn tractors and agricultural machinery.

OPERATING INFORMATION

Opening Times: 2015 dates: Saturdays, Sundays and Bank Holiday Mondays from 28th March to 28th June and on weekends during September. Open daily during July and August. Trains usually run from 12.30pm to 4.00pm. Santa Specials operate during the first two weekends in December when higher fares apply.

Steam Working: None at present
Prices: Adult Return £4.50
Child Return £3.50
Family 'Weekly Pass' £20.00
Season Ticket £40.00

Detailed Directions by Car:
From All Parts: Alford is situated 25 miles west of Aberdeen on the Highland tourist route. Take the A944 to reach Alford.

ALMOND VALLEY LIGHT RAILWAY

Address: Almond Valley Heritage Centre, Millfield, Livingston EH54 7AR
Telephone N°: (01506) 414957
Year Formed: 1993
Location of Line: Livingston
Length of Line: 550 yards

N° of Steam Locos: None
N° of Other Locos: 3
Approx N° of Visitors P.A.: 125,000
Gauge: 2 feet 6 inches
Web site: www.almondvalley.co.uk
E-mail: rac@almondvalley.co.uk

GENERAL INFORMATION

Nearest Mainline Station: Livingston North (1 mile)
Nearest Bus Station: Livingston (1 mile)
Car Parking: Available on site
Coach Parking: Available
Souvenir Shop(s): Yes
Food & Drinks: Available

SPECIAL INFORMATION

The railway runs through the grounds of the Almond Valley Heritage Centre which hosts a wide range of other attractions including a farm, a historic Mill, nature trails and picnic areas.

OPERATING INFORMATION

Opening Times: The Centre is open daily throughout the year but for 25th & 26th December and 1st & 2nd January. The railway operates at weekends between Easter and the end of September, and daily during some holiday periods, from 11.00am to 4.00pm. Please contact Almond Valley for further details.
Steam Working: None at present.
Prices: Adults £6.50 (Admission to Centre)
     Children £5.00 (Admission to Centre)
     Family £19.00 (Admission to Centre)
Note: Train rides are an extra £1.00 per person.

Detailed Directions by Car:
From All Parts: Exit the M8 at Junction 3A and take the A779 towards Livingston. Almond Valley Heritage Centre is located near the junction of the A779 and the A705 and is clearly signposted.

AMBERLEY MUSEUM & HERITAGE CENTRE

Address: Amberley Museum & Heritage
Centre, Amberley, Arundel   BN18 9LT
Telephone Nº: (01798) 831370
E-mail: office@amberleymuseum.co.uk
Year Formed: 1979
Location of Line: Amberley
Length of Line: ¾ mile

Nº of Steam Locos: 3
Nº of Other Locos: 20+
Nº of Members: 300 volunteers
Annual Membership Fee: £25.00
Approx Nº of Visitors P.A.: 40,000
Gauge: 2 feet
Web site: www.amberleymuseum.co.uk

GENERAL INFORMATION

Nearest Mainline Station: Amberley (adjacent)
Nearest Bus Station: –
Car Parking: Free parking available on site
Coach Parking: Free parking available on site
Souvenir Shop(s): Yes
Food & Drinks: Yes

SPECIAL INFORMATION

Amberley Museum covers 36 acres of former chalk
pits and comprises over 30 buildings containing
hundreds of different exhibits.

OPERATING INFORMATION

Opening Times: 2015 dates: Wednesday to Sunday
from 4th March to 1st November and also on Bank
Holiday Mondays. Open daily in August and during
other local School Holidays. Trains operate from
approximately 11.00am until 4.00pm
Steam Working: Please phone for details.
Prices: Adult £11.00
          Child £6.60 (free for Under-4's)
          Concessions £10.00
          Family £33.00 (2 adults + 3 children)

Detailed Directions by Car:
From All Parts: Amberley Museum is situated in West Sussex on the B2139 mid-way between Arundel and
Storrington and is adjacent to Amberley Railway Station.

AMERTON RAILWAY

Address: Amerton Farm, Stow-by-Chartley, Staffordshire ST18 0LA	**Nº of Steam Locos**: 2 (+2 in restoration)
	Nº of Other Locos: 6 (+2 in restoration)
Telephone Nº: (01889) 271337	**Nº of Members**: 90
Year Formed: 1991	**Approx Nº of Visitors P.A.**: 30,000
Location: Amerton Farm	**Gauge**: 2 feet
Length of Line: Approximately 1 mile	**Web site**: www.amertonrailway.co.uk

GENERAL INFORMATION

Nearest Mainline Station: Stafford (8 miles)
Nearest Bus Station: Stafford (8 miles)
Car Parking: Free parking available on site
Coach Parking: Available by arrangement
Souvenir Shop(s): Yes
Food & Drinks: Yes

SPECIAL INFORMATION

The railway operates both locomotives and rolling stock which was built in Staffordshire. The Summer Steam Gala in 2015 will be held on 20th & 21st June.

OPERATING INFORMATION

Opening Times: 2015 dates: Weekends from the 21st March to 1st November and daily during the School Holidays. Santa Specials run on weekends from 28th November to 20th December. Open from 11.30am to 4.30pm at weekends but only until 4.00pm during midweek dates.
Steam Working: Sundays and Bank Holidays plus some other Special Events. Please contact the railway for further information.
Prices: Adult £2.20 Child £1.50
Concession £1.70
E-mail: enquiries@amertonrailway.co.uk

Detailed Directions by Car:
Amerton is located on the A518, 1 mile from the junction with the A51 – Amerton Farm is signposted at the junction. The Railway is located approximately 8 miles from Junction 14 of the M6.

APEDALE VALLEY LIGHT RAILWAY

Address: Apedale Valley Country Park, Chesterton, Newcastle-under-Lyme
Telephone Nº: 0845 094-1953
Year Formed: 1969
Location: Apedale Valley Community Country Park
Length of Line: ¼ mile

Nº of Steam Locos: 3
Nº of Other Locos: 67
Nº of Members: 200+
Annual Membership Fee: £17.00
Gauge: 2 feet
Web site: www.avlr.org.uk

GENERAL INFORMATION

Nearest Mainline Station: Longport (2 miles)
Nearest Bus Station: Hanley (3½ miles)
Car Parking: Available
Coach Parking: Available
Souvenir Shop(s): Yes
Food & Drinks: Available

SPECIAL INFORMATION

The Apedale Valley Light Railway is operated by the Moseley Railway Trust (www.mrt.org.uk).

OPERATING INFORMATION

Opening Times: 2015 dates: Saturdays, Bank Holidays and some Sundays from 5th April to 8th November. Santa Specials run on some weekends in December. Trains usually run from 11.30am to 4.00pm. Please contact the railway for further information.
Steam Working: Special Event days, Bank Holiday Sundays and Mondays plus the second weekend in each month from April to November (but the third weekend in May).
Prices: Adult £2.50
Child £1.50
Note: Different prices may apply for special events.

Detailed Directions by Car:
Exit the M6 at Junction 16 and take the A500 to the A34 and head southwards. Turn right at the traffic island by the McDonald's restaurant and follow the brown tourist signs for Apedale Valley. Follow Loomer Road in Chesterton to the end and continue into the Park. Use the car park at the Heritage Centre as there is no direct access to the railway by car. SatNav: Use ST5 7LB. This postcode is the speedway track on the approach to the park. Continue past the speedway track and continue along Loomer Road for the park.

ASTLEY GREEN COLLIERY MUSEUM

Address: Higher Green Lane,
Astley Green, Tyldesley   M29 7JB
Telephone Nº: (01942) 708969
Year Formed: 1983
Location of Line: Astley Green Colliery
Length of Line: 440 yards

Nº of Steam Locos: None
Nº of Other Locos: 33
Nº of Members: 120
Approx Nº of Visitors P.A.: 6,000
Gauge: 2 feet
Web site: www.agcm.org.uk

GENERAL INFORMATION

Nearest Mainline Station: Salford (3 miles)
Nearest Bus Station: Manchester (5 miles)
Car Parking: Available on site
Coach Parking: Available
Souvenir Shop(s): None
Food & Drinks: None

SPECIAL INFORMATION

Astley Green Colliery Museum houses the largest
collection of underground colliery locos in the UK.
The 440 yard line is used for freight demonstrations.

OPERATING INFORMATION

Opening Times: Tuesday, Thursday, Saturday and
Sunday throughout the year except for Christmas
Day and Boxing Day. Also open at other times by
prior arrangement. Open from 1.30pm to 5.00pm.
Steam Working: None
Prices: No admission charge but donations are
gratefully accepted.
Note: The museum does not offer passenger rides.

Detailed Directions by Car:
From All Parts: Exit the M6 at Junction 23 and take the A580 towards Manchester. After about 6 miles cross the
Bridgewater Canal then take the next right signposted Higher Green. After approximately ¼ mile turn left into
the Colliery grounds.

AUDLEY END STEAM RAILWAY

Address: Audley End, Saffron Walden, Essex
Telephone Nº: (01799) 542134
Year Formed: 1964
Location of Line: Opposite Audley End House, Saffron Walden

Length of Line: 1½ miles
Nº of Steam Locos: 5
Nº of Other Locos: 2
Approx Nº of Visitors P.A.: 42,000
Gauge: 10¼ inches
Web site: www.audley-end-railway.co.uk

GENERAL INFORMATION

Nearest Mainline Station: Audley End (1 mile)
Nearest Bus Station: Saffron Walden (1 mile)
Car Parking: Available on site
Coach Parking: Available on site
Souvenir Shop(s): Yes
Food & Drinks: Available in the Cafe

SPECIAL INFORMATION

Audley End Steam Railway is Lord Braybrooke's private miniature railway situated just next to Audley End House, an English Heritage site. Private parties can be catered for outside of normal running hours.

OPERATING INFORMATION

Opening Times: 2015 dates: Weekends and Bank Holidays from 28th March to 18th October and also daily during the School Holidays. Santa Specials operate on 28th & 29th November and 5th, 6th, 12th, 13th and 16th to 24th December. Trains run from 12.00pm (11.00am on Bank Holidays) until approximately 4.45pm.
Steam Working: Weekends and Bank Holidays.
Prices: Adult Return £5.50
Child Return £4.50 (Under-2s ride free)
Santa Specials £8.00
Note: Multi-ride tickets are also available.

Detailed Directions by Car:
Exit the M11 at Junction 10 if southbound or Junction 9 if northbound and follow the signs for Audley End House. The railway is situated just across the road from Audley End House.

BALA LAKE RAILWAY

Address: Bala Lake Railway, Llanuwchllyn, Gwynedd, LL23 7DD **Telephone Nº**: (01678) 540666 **Year Formed**: 1972 **Location of Line**: Llanuwchllyn to Bala **Length of Line**: 4½ miles	**Nº of Steam Locos**: 5 (all are not in **Nº of Other Locos**: 3 working order) **Approx Nº of Visitors P.A.**: 20,000 **Gauge**: 1 foot 11 five-eighth inches **Web site**: www.bala-lake-railway.co.uk **E-mail**: balalake@btconnect.com

GENERAL INFORMATION

Nearest Mainline Station: Wrexham (40 miles)
Nearest Bus Station: Wrexham (40 miles)
Car Parking: Adequate parking in Llanuwchllyn
Coach Parking: At Llanuwchllyn or in Bala Town Centre
Souvenir Shop(s): Yes
Food & Drinks: Yes – unlicensed!

SPECIAL INFORMATION

Bala Lake Railway is a narrow-gauge railway which follows 4½ miles of the former Ruabon to Barmouth G.W.R. line.

OPERATING INFORMATION

Opening Times: Easter until the end of September but closed on Mondays and Fridays (excepting Bank Holidays) in April, May, June and September. Also open on some dates during October.
Steam Working: All advertised services are steam hauled. Trains run from 11.15am to 3.45pm.
Prices: Adult Single £6.50;   Return £9.50
Child Single £3.00;   Return £5.00
Senior Citizen Return £9.00
Family Tickets (Return): £12.00 (1 Adult + 1 Child);
£24.00 (2 Adults + 2 Children).
Additional Children are charged £3.00 each.
Under-3s travel free of charge.

Detailed Directions by Car:
From All Parts: The railway is situated off the A494 Bala to Dolgellau road which is accessible from the national motorways via the A5 or A55.

BICKINGTON STEAM RAILWAY

Address: Trago Mills Shopping & Leisure Centre, Stover, Devon   TQ12 6JB
Telephone Nº: (01626) 821111
Year Formed: 1988
Location of Line: Near the junction of A38 and A382
Length of Line: 2½ miles

Nº of Steam Locos: 4
Nº of Other Locos: 1
Approx Nº of Visitors P.A.: Not known
Gauge: 10¼ inches
Web site: freespace.virgin.net/ hanson.mike/Tragorailway.htm

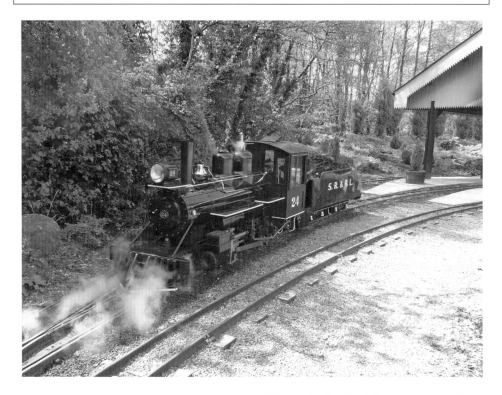

GENERAL INFORMATION

Nearest Mainline Station: Newton Abbott (3½ miles)
Nearest Bus Station: Newton Abbott
Car Parking: Free parking available on site
Coach Parking: Available on site
Souvenir Shop(s): Yes
Food & Drinks: Available adjacent to the Railway

SPECIAL INFORMATION

Bickington Steam Railway is part of the Trago Mills Shopping & Leisure Centre which occupies around 100 acres of rolling South Devon countryside. The site has numerous other attractions including, 'The Finest 00-gauge Model Railway in the UK'!

OPERATING INFORMATION

Opening Times: Monday to Saturday 11.00am to 5.00pm and Sundays 12.00pm to 4.00pm.
Steam Working: Most operating days but please contact the Railway for precise information.
Prices: Adult Day Rover £4.99
      Child Day Rover £3.99

Detailed Directions by Car:
From All Parts: Take the M5 from Exeter to the A38 and head towards Plymouth. Exit at the junction with the A382 and follow the signs for 'Trago Mills'. The railway is situated on this road after about 1 mile.

BICTON WOODLAND RAILWAY

Address: Bicton Woodland Railway, Bicton Park Botanical Gardens, East Budleigh, Budleigh Salterton   EX9 7OP
Telephone Nº: (01395) 568465
Year Formed: 1963
Location of Line: Bicton Gardens
Length of Line: 1½ miles

Nº of Steam Locos: None at present
Nº of Other Locos: 3
Nº of Members: 15,000
Annual Membership Fee: From £14.00
Approx Nº of Visitors P.A.: 300,000
Gauge: 1 foot 6 inches
Web site: www.bictongardens.co.uk

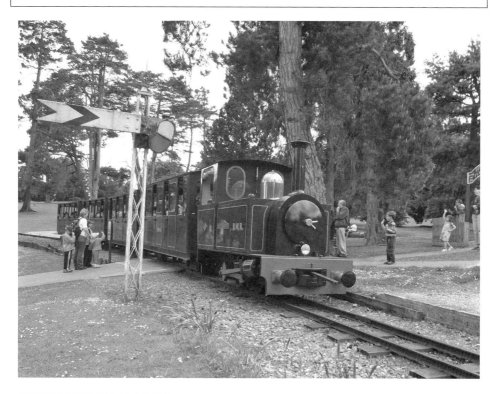

GENERAL INFORMATION

Nearest Railtrack Station: Exmouth (6 miles)
Nearest Bus Station: Exeter (14 miles)
Car Parking: Free parking at site
Coach Parking: Free parking at site
Souvenir Shop(s): Yes
Food & Drinks: Yes

SPECIAL INFORMATION

The railway runs through the grounds of Bicton Park Botanical Gardens which span over 60 acres. The railway is the only 18 inch gauge line in the UK.

OPERATING INFORMATION

Opening Times: Daily 10.00am to 5.30pm during the Summer and 10.00am to 4.30pm during the Winter. Closed on Christmas Day and Boxing Day.
Steam Working: None at present
Prices: Adult £8.95 (Entrance);   £1.90 (Rides)
Child £6.95 (Entrance);   £1.50 (Rides)
Concessions £7.95 (Entrance);   £1.70 (Rides)

Detailed Directions by Car:
From All Parts: Exit the M5 motorway at Exeter services, Junction 30 and follow the brown tourist signs to Bicton Park.

BRECON MOUNTAIN RAILWAY

Address: Pant Station, Merthyr Tydfil, CF48 2UP	**Gauge:** 1 foot 11¾ inches
Telephone Nº: (01685) 722988	**Length of Line:** 5 miles
Year Formed: 1980	**Nº of Steam Locos:** 8
Location of Line: North of Merthyr Tydfil – 1 mile from the A465	**Nº of Other Locos:** 3
	Approx Nº of Visitors P.A.: 75,000
	Web: www.breconmountainrailway.co.uk

GENERAL INFORMATION

Nearest Mainline Station: Merthyr Tydfil (3 miles)
Nearest Bus Station: Merthyr Tydfil (3 miles)
Car Parking: Free parking available at Pant Station
Coach Parking: Free parking available at Pant Station
Souvenir Shop(s): Yes
Food & Drinks: Yes – including licensed Tea Rooms

SPECIAL INFORMATION

It is possible to take a break before the return journey at Pontsticill to have a picnic, take a forest walk, visit the lakeside snackbar and play area or visit the new Steam Museum.

OPERATING INFORMATION

Opening Times: Weekends and Bank Holidays throughout the year and daily during School holidays. Daily from the start of April to the end of October but closed on some Mondays and Fridays in April, May, September and October. Open almost every day in December for Santa Specials. Trains typically run from 10.30am to 3.45pm and from 12.00pm to 3.00pm during off-peak times.
Steam Working: Most services are steam hauled.
Prices: Adults £12.00
Children £6.00 (Ages 2 and under ride free)
Senior Citizens £10.75
Note: Two children can travel for £5.00 each when accompanying a paying adult.

Detailed Directions by Car:
Exit the M4 at Junction 32 and take the A470 to Merthyr Tydfil. Go onto the A465 and follow the brown tourist signs for the railway. SATNAV users should enter the following postcode: CF48 2DD

BREDGAR & WORMSHILL LIGHT RAILWAY

Address: The Warren, Bredgar, near Sittingbourne, Kent ME9 8AT	**Gauge**: 2 feet
Telephone Nº: (01622) 884254	**Nº of Steam Locos**: 10
Year Formed: 1972	**Nº of Other Locos**: 5
Location of Line: 1 mile south of Bredgar	**Approx Nº of Visitors P.A.**: 7,000
Length of Line: ¾ mile	**Web site**: www.bwlr.co.uk

GENERAL INFORMATION

Nearest Mainline Station: Sittingbourne (5 miles)
Nearest Bus Station: Sittingbourne
Car Parking: 500 spaces available – free parking
Coach Parking: Free parking available by appointment
Souvenir Shop(s): Yes   **Food & Drinks**: Yes

SPECIAL INFORMATION

A small but beautiful railway in rural Kent. The railway also has other attractions including a Model Railway, Traction Engines, a working Beam Engine, Vintage cars and tractors, a Locomotive Shed, a picnic site and woodland walks.

OPERATING INFORMATION

Opening Times: 2015 dates: Open on Easter Sunday then the first Sunday of the month from May to October and on Sunday 25th October. Trains run from 11.00am to 4.30pm.
Steam Working: Please contact the railway for further information.
Prices: Adult £10.00
             Child £4.00 (Under-4s travel free)
             Family Ticket £25.00
                        (2 adults + 3 children)
Note: The prices shown above include parking and unlimited rides on the day of purchase.

Detailed Directions by Car:
Take the M20 and exit at Junction 8 (Leeds Castle exit). Travel 4½ miles due north through Hollingbourne. The Railway is situated a little over 1 mile south of Bredgar village.

BURE VALLEY RAILWAY

Address: Aylsham Station, Norwich Road, Aylsham, Norfolk NR11 6BW	**Nº of Steam Locos:** 5
Telephone Nº: (01263) 733858	**Nº of Other Locos:** 3
Year Formed: 1989	**Approx Nº of Visitors P.A.:** 120,000
Location of Line: Aylsham to Wroxham	**Gauge:** 15 inches
Length of Line: 9 miles	**Web Site:** www.bvrw.co.uk
	e-mail: info@bvrw.co.uk

GENERAL INFORMATION

Nearest Mainline Station: Wroxham (adjacent)
Nearest Bus Station: Aylsham (bus passes station)
Car Parking: Free parking for passengers at Aylsham and Wroxham Stations
Coach Parking: As above
Souvenir Shop(s): Yes at both Stations
Food & Drinks: Yes (Café at Aylsham opens daily)

SPECIAL INFORMATION

Boat trains connect at Wroxham with a 1½ hour cruise on the Norfolk Broads National Park. Steam Locomotive driving courses are available throughout the year except in July and August. Some carriages are able to carry wheelchairs.

OPERATING INFORMATION

Opening Times: Aylsham Station is open daily. Trains run on various dates in 2015 including weekends in March and November and daily from 28th March to 1st November, plus some other dates. Trains run from 10.00am to 5.25pm during high season. Open for Santa Specials on weekends and other dates in November and December. Trains also operate from 27th December to 3rd January and during the February half-term.
Please contact the railway for further details.
Steam Working: Most trains are steam hauled
Prices: Adult Return £12.50 (Single £8.00)
Child Return £6.50 (Single £5.00)
Family Return £33.00 (2 adult + 2 child)
Party discounts are available for groups of 20 or more if booked in advance.

Detailed Directions by Car:
From Norwich: Aylsham Station is situated midway between Norwich and Cromer on the A140 – follow the signs for Aylsham Town Centre. Wroxham Station is adjacent to the Wroxham British Rail Station – take the A1151 from Norwich; From King's Lynn: Take the A148 and B1354 to reach Aylsham Station.
Satellite Navigation: Use NR11 6BW for Aylsham Station and NR12 8UU for Wroxham Station.

CLEETHORPES COAST LIGHT RAILWAY

Address: King's Road, Cleethorpes, North East Lincolnshire DN35 0AG
Telephone Nº: (01472) 604657
Year Formed: 1948
Location of Line: Lakeside Park & Marine embankment along Cleethorpes seafront
Length of Line: Almost 2 miles

Nº of Steam Locos: 8
Nº of Other Locos: 5
Nº of Members: 200
Annual Membership Fee: Adult £11.00
Approx Nº of Visitors P.A.: 120,000
Gauge: 15 inches
Web: www.cleethorpescoastlightrailway.co.uk

GENERAL INFORMATION

Nearest Mainline Station: Cleethorpes (1 mile)
Nearest Bus Stop: Meridian Point (opposite)
Car Parking: Boating Lake car park – 500 spaces (fee charged)
Coach Parking: As above
Souvenir Shop(s): Yes
Food & Drinks: Brief Encounters Cafe and The Signal Box Inn are both located at Lakeside Station.

E-mail: info@cleethorpescoastlightrailway.co.uk

OPERATING INFORMATION

Opening Times: 2015 dates: Open on weekends, Bank Holidays and during School Holidays throughout the year. Open daily from Easter to early September. 'Hallowscream Express' trains run on dates in October and Santa Specials operate during December. Trains run from 10.00am to 6.00pm in the Summer months and from 10.50am to 4.20pm in the Winter months. Please contact the railway for further information.
Steam Working: Most services are steam hauled.
Prices: Adult Return £4.00
Child Return £3.50
Family Return £12.00   (2 Adult + 2 Child)
Note: Lower prices apply for shorter journeys and Under-3s travel free

---

Detailed Directions by Car:
Take the M180 to the A180 and continue to its' end. Follow signs for Cleethorpes. The Railway is situated along Cleethorpes seafront 1 mile to the south of the Pier. Look for the brown tourist signs marked Meridian Lakeside and the main station is adjacent to the Leisure Centre.

THE CORRIS RAILWAY

Address: Station Yard, Corris, Machynlleth, Mid Wales SY20 9SH **Telephone Nº**: (01654) 761303 **Year Formed**: 1966 **Location of Line**: Corris to Maespoeth, Mid Wales **Length of Line**: ¾ mile	**Nº of Steam Locos**: 1 **Nº of Other Locos**: 5 **Nº of Members**: 500 **Annual Membership Fee**: £20.00 (adult) **Approx Nº of Visitors P.A.**: 7,000 **Gauge**: 2 feet 3 inches **Web site**: www.corris.co.uk **E-mail**: enquiries@corris.co.uk

GENERAL INFORMATION

Nearest Mainline Station: Machynlleth (5 miles)
Nearest Bus Station: Machynlleth (5 miles)
Car Parking: Available on site and also at the Corris Craft Centre (500 yards)
Coach Parking: Corris Craft Centre (please pre-book if visiting)
Souvenir Shop(s): Yes
Food & Drinks: Yes

SPECIAL INFORMATION

The Corris Railway originally ran from 1859 to 1948. A second locomotive and three carriages are currently being built and work on an extension to the partly-rebuilt line is currently underway.

OPERATING INFORMATION

Opening Times: 2015 dates: Open during Easter Weekend then every Sunday from 2nd May to 27th September, some Saturdays in May, all Saturdays in July and August, Mondays and Tuesdays during August, on all Bank Holiday weekends and on 24th & 25th October. Santa Specials run on 12th & 13th December. The first train leaves Corris Station at 11.00am, the last train leaves at 4.00pm.
Steam Working: Most trains are steam-hauled.
Prices: Adult Return £6.00
          Child Return £3.00 (Ages 5 to 15)
          Senior Citizen Return £5.50
          Family Return £15.00
                  (2 adults + 2 children)

Detailed Directions by Car:
From All Parts: Corris is situated off the A487, five miles north of Machynlleth and 11 miles south of Dolgellau. Turn off the trunk road at the Braichgoch Bunkhouse & Inn and the Station Yard is the 2nd turning on the right as you enter the village, just past the Holy Trinity Church.

DERBYSHIRE DALES NARROW GAUGE RAILWAY

Correspondence: 44 Midland Terrace, Westhouses, Alfreton   DE55 5AB
Contact Phone Nº: (01629) 580381
Year Formed: 1998
Location of Line: Rowsley South Station, Peak Rail (SATNAV use DE4 2LF)
Length of Line: 500 yards

Nº of Steam Locos: None
Nº of Other Locos: 8
Approx Nº of Visitors P.A.: 1,687 (2014)
Gauge: 2 feet
Web site: www.peakrail.co.uk

GENERAL INFORMATION

Nearest Mainline Station: Matlock (4 miles)
Nearest Bus Station: Matlock (4 miles)
Car Parking: 200 spaces at Rowsley South Station
Coach Parking: Free parking at Rowsley South
Souvenir Shop(s): Yes
Food & Drinks: Yes

SPECIAL INFORMATION

This narrow gauge line is operated at Peak Rail's Rowsley South Station. The line has now been extended to 500 yards. Holders of valid Peak Rail tickets can travel free for one return journey.

OPERATING INFORMATION

Opening Times: Sundays and Bank Holiday weekends from April to early October. Also open on certain Wednesdays in July and August. A total of 30 operating days. Please contact the railway for further information.
Steam Working: None at present.
Prices: Adult £1.00
             Children 50p

Detailed Directions by Car:
Follow the A6 Bakewell to Matlock road to Rowsley then follow the brown tourist signs for the Peak Rail Station.

DEVON RAILWAY CENTRE

Address: Bickleigh, Tiverton, Devon, EX16 8RG	**Nº of Steam Locos**: 1
Telephone Nº: (01884) 855671	**Nº of Other Locos**: 12
Year Formed: 1997	**Approx Nº of Visitors P.A.**: Not recorded
Location of Line: Bickleigh, Devon	**Gauge**: 2 feet, 7¼ inches and Standard
Length of Line: ½ mile (2 foot and 7¼ inch gauges); 200 yards (Standard gauge)	**Web site**: www.devonrailwaycentre.co.uk
	E-mail: devonrailway@btinternet.com

GENERAL INFORMATION

Nearest Mainline Station: Exeter
Nearest Bus Station: Tiverton (Route 55)
Car Parking: Available on site
Coach Parking: Available on site
Souvenir Shop(s): Yes
Food & Drinks: Yes

SPECIAL INFORMATION

Devon Railway Centre has passenger carrying lines and also features a large model railway exhibition with 15 working layouts. A delightful Edwardian model village built to a 1:12 scale has recently been extended with a model funfair added.

OPERATING INFORMATION

Opening Times: 2015 dates: Daily from 28th March to 12th April, 20th May to 6th September and 24th October to 1st November. Closed on Mondays in June. Open Wednesday to Sunday inclusive from 6th to 17th May and 9th to 27th September and also during weekends in April and October. Open from 10.30am until 5.00pm on all operating days.
Steam Working: Trains may be steam or diesel hauled so please phone for further details.
Prices: Adult £7.95   Child £6.90
    Senior Citizen £7.20   Family £27.00
Admission includes unlimited train rides and access to the model village, model railways and museum.

Detailed Directions by Car:
From All Parts: Devon Railway Centre is situated adjacent to the famous Bickleigh Bridge, just off the A396 Exeter to Tiverton road (3 miles from Tiverton and 8 miles from Exeter).

EASTLEIGH LAKESIDE STEAM RAILWAY

Address: Lakeside Country Park,
Wide Lane, Eastleigh, Hants. SO50 5PE
Telephone Nº: (023) 8061-2020
Year Formed: 1992
Location: Opposite Southampton airport
Length of Line: 1¼ miles

Nº of Steam Locos: 20
Nº of Other Locos: 3
Approx Nº of Visitors P.A.: 50,000
Gauge: 10¼ inches and 7¼ inches
Web site: www.steamtrain.co.uk

GENERAL INFORMATION

Nearest Mainline Station: Southampton Airport
(Parkway) (¼ mile)
Nearest Bus Station: Eastleigh (1½ miles)
Car Parking: Free parking available on site
Coach Parking: Free parking available on site
Souvenir Shop(s): Yes
Food & Drinks: Cafe on site is open all year round
from 9.00am to 4.00pm.

SPECIAL INFORMATION

The railway also has a playground and picnic area
overlooking the lakes.

OPERATING INFORMATION

Opening Times: Weekends throughout the year and
daily during school holidays. Open 10.00am to
4.30pm (until 4.00pm during the winter months).
Santa Specials run on some dates in December.
Steam Working: As above
Prices: Adult Return £3.50 (First Class £4.00)
Child Return £2.50 (First Class £3.00)
Tickets are available offering 3 return journeys at
reduced rates. Annual season tickets are available.
Children under the age of 2 years ride free of charge.
Driver training courses can be booked in advance.

Detailed Directions by Car:
From All Parts: Exit the M27 at Junction 5 and take the A335 to Eastleigh. The Railway is situated ¼ mile past
Southampton Airport Station on the left hand side of the A335.

EAST SUFFOLK LIGHT RAILWAY

Address: East Anglia Transport Museum,
Chapel Road, Carlton Colville,
Lowestoft NR33 8BL
Telephone Nº: (01502) 518459
Year Formed: 1972
Location: 3 miles south of Lowestoft
Length of Line: 200 yards

Nº of Steam Locos: None
Nº of Other Locos: 4
Approx Nº of Visitors P.A.: 18,000
Gauge: 2 feet
Web site: www.eatm.org.uk

GENERAL INFORMATION

Nearest Mainline Station: Oulton Broad South
(2 miles)
Nearest Bus Station: Lowestoft (3 miles)
Car Parking: Available on site
Coach Parking: Available
Souvenir Shop(s): Yes
Food & Drinks: Available

SPECIAL INFORMATION

The railway is located at the East Anglia Transport
Museum which also offers visitors trolleybus and
tram rides.

OPERATING INFORMATION

Opening Times: 2015 dates: Sundays and
Thursdays from April to September, also Saturdays
from June to September, Tuesdays and Wednesdays
from 21st July to 30th August and some other dates.
Open from 1.00pm to 5.00pm on most days but
from 11.00am to 5.00pm on Sundays and Bank
Holidays.
Steam Working: None
Prices: Adults £8.00 (Admission and all rides)
Children £6.00 (Admission and all rides)
Concessions £7.00 (Admission and rides)

Detailed Directions by Car:
From All Parts: The East Anglia Transport Museum is clearly signposted by brown tourist signs from the A12,
A146, A1117 and A1145.

EVESHAM VALE LIGHT RAILWAY

Address: Evesham Country Park, Twyford, Evesham WR11 4TP	**Nº of Steam Locos:** 3
Telephone Nº: (01386) 422282	**Nº of Other Locos:** 2
Year Formed: 2002	**Approx Nº of Visitors P.A.:** 50,000
Location of Line: 1 mile north of Evesham	**Gauge:** 15 inches
Length of Line: 1¼ miles	**Web site:** www.evlr.co.uk
	E-mail: enquiries@evlr.co.uk

GENERAL INFORMATION

Nearest Mainline Station: Evesham (1 mile)
Nearest Bus Station: Evesham (1½ miles)
Car Parking: Available in the Country Park
Coach Parking: Available in the Country Park
Souvenir Shop(s): Yes
Food & Drinks: Restaurant at the Garden Centre

SPECIAL INFORMATION

The railway is situated within the 130 acre Evesham Country Park which has apple orchards and picnic areas overlooking the picturesque Vale of Evesham.

OPERATING INFORMATION

Opening Times: Open at weekends throughout the year and daily during school holidays. Trains run from 10.30am to 5.00pm (until 4.00pm during the winter). Please phone for further details.
Steam Working: Daily when trains are running.
Prices: Adult Return   £2.40
                Child Return   £1.80
                Senior Citizen Return   £2.10
Note: Special reduced party rates are available for groups of 20 or more when booked in advance.

Detailed Directions by Car:
From the North: Exit the M42 at Junction 3 and take the A435 towards Alcester then the A46 to Evesham; From the South: Exit the M5 at Junction 9 and take the A46 to Evesham; From the West: Exit the M5 at Junction 7 and take the A44 to Evesham; From the East: Take the A44 from Oxford to Evesham. Upon reaching Evesham, follow the Brown tourist signs for Evesham Country Park and the railway.

EXBURY GARDENS RAILWAY

Address: Exbury Gardens, Exbury,
Near Southampton   SO45 1AZ
Telephone Nº: (02380) 891203
Year Formed: 2001
Location of Line: Exbury
Length of Line: 1¼ miles

Nº of Steam Locos: 3
Nº of Other Locos: 1
Approx Nº of Visitors P.A.: 55,000
Gauge: 12¼ inches
Web site: www.exbury.co.uk

Photograph courtesy of Gavin Clinton

GENERAL INFORMATION

Nearest Mainline Station: Brockenhurst (8 miles)
Nearest Bus Station: Hill Top (2½ miles)
The New Forest Open Tour Bus visits the gardens 8
times a day between 29th June and 15th September.
Car Parking: Free parking available on site
Coach Parking: Free parking available on site
Souvenir Shop(s): Yes
Food & Drinks: Available

SPECIAL INFORMATION

The railway is located in the world famous Rothschild
azalea and rhododendron gardens at Exbury in the
New Forest. A walk-through exhibition in the Engine
Shed recalls the building of the steam railway.

OPERATING INFORMATION

Opening Times: 2015 dates: Daily from the 14th
March to 1st November. The gardens are open from
10.00am to 5.00pm (or dusk if earlier) and car park
gates close at 6.00pm.
Steam Working: Most running days from 11.00am
(restricted operation in March and September).
Prices: Adult Return £4.00
            Child Return £4.00   (Under-3s free)
Note: The above prices do not include admission to
the Gardens which is required to visit the railway.
Please check the Exbury web site for further details
of entrance fees for the Gardens.

Detailed Directions by Car:
From all directions: Exit the M27 at Junction 2 and take the A326 to Dibden. Follow the brown tourist signs for
Exbury Gardens & Steam Railway.

FAIRBOURNE RAILWAY

Address: Beach Road, Fairbourne,
Dolgellau, Gwynedd LL38 2EX
Telephone Nº: (01341) 250362
Year Formed: 1916
Location of Line: On A493 between
Tywyn & Dolgellau
Length of Line: 2 miles

Nº of Steam Locos: 4
Nº of Other Locos: 2
Nº of Members: 400
Annual Membership Fee: £25.00
Approx Nº of Visitors P.A.: 18,000
Gauge: 12¼ inches
Web Site: www.fairbournerailway.com

GENERAL INFORMATION

Nearest Mainline Station: Fairbourne (adjacent)
Nearest Bus Station: Fairbourne (adjacent)
Car Parking: Available in Mainline station car park
Coach Parking: Pay & Display car park 300 yards
Souvenir Shop(s): Yes
Food & Drinks: Yes – licensed Cafes at Fairbourne
and Barmouth Ferry Terminus

SPECIAL INFORMATION

There is a connecting ferry service (foot passengers
only) from Barmouth to Barmouth Ferry Terminus.

E-mail: fairbourne.rail@btconnect.com

OPERATING INFORMATION

Opening Times: 2015 dates: Open daily from 28th
March until 29th October but closed on Mondays
and Fridays except during the School Holidays. The
Little to Large Gala with an intensive timetable is on
24th & 25th May which features the 15-inch gauge
visiting engines. Santa Specials run on 19th and 20th
December.
Steam Working: The majority of services are
steam-hauled.
Prices: Adult Return £9.50
 Unaccompanied Child Return £5.25
  (accompanied Children are £1.00 each)
 Senior Citizen Return £8.50

Detailed Directions by Car:
From A470: Follow signs for Dolgellau and turn left onto A493 towards Tywyn. The turn-off for Fairbourne is
located 8 miles south-west of Dolgellau; From South Wales: Follow signs for Machynlleth, then follow A487
towards Dolgellau. Then take A493 towards Fairbourne.

FAVERSHAM MINIATURE RAILWAY

Address: Brogdale Farm, Brogdale Road, Faversham, Kent ME13 8XZ
Telephone Nº: (01795) 474211
Year Formed: 1984
Location of Line: Faversham, Kent
Length of Line: 1 mile
Gauge: 9 inches

Nº of Steam Locos: 3
Nº of Other Locos: 9
Nº of Members: 40
Annual Membership Fee: £10.00 Adult, £40.00 Family
Approx Nº of Visitors P.A.: 6,000+
Web: www.favershamminiaturerailway.co.uk

GENERAL INFORMATION

Nearest Mainline Station: Faversham (¾ mile)
Nearest Bus Station: None, but a regular bus service travels to Faversham from Canterbury
Car Parking: Available on site
Coach Parking: Available on site
Souvenir Shop(s): Various shops on site
Food & Drinks: Available

SPECIAL INFORMATION

Faversham Miniature Railway is the only 9 inch gauge railway in the UK which is open to the public.

OPERATING INFORMATION

Opening Times: Sundays and Bank Holiday weekends from early March to November from 11.00am to 4.00pm. Also open for Santa Specials and other Special Events during the year. Please contact the railway for further information.
Steam Working: Special steam days only. Please contact the Railway for further details.
Prices: £1.50 per ride
£2.00 per ride when Steam-hauled

Detailed Directions by Car:
Exit the M2 at Junction 5 and take the A251 towards Faversham. After about ½ mile turn left onto the A2 then left again after ¼ mile turning into Brogdale Road for the Farm and Railway.

Ferry Meadows Miniature Railway

Address: Ham Lane, Nene Park,
Oundle Road, Peterborough   PE2 5UU
Telephone Nº: (01933) 398889
Year Formed: 1978
Location: Ferry Meadows, Nene Park
Length of Line: ½ mile

Nº of Steam Locos: 1
Nº of Other Locos: 2
Approx Nº of Visitors P.A.: 40,000
Gauge: 10¼ inches
Web site: www.ferrymeadowsrailway.co.uk

GENERAL INFORMATION

Nearest Mainline Station: Peterborough (2 miles)
Nearest Bus Station: Peterborough (2 miles)
Car Parking: Available adjacent
Coach Parking: Available adjacent
Souvenir Shop(s): Yes
Food & Drinks: Available

SPECIAL INFORMATION

The railway is situated in the Ferry Meadows area of
Nene Park in which watersports and other leisure
activities are also available.

OPERATING INFORMATION

Opening Times: 2015 dates: Every weekend from
1st March to 1st November and daily during the
school holidays.
Trains run from 11.30am to 4.30pm.
Steam Working: Every Sunday and some weekdays
during the School Holidays. Please contact the
railway for further details.
Prices: Adult Return £2.50   Adult Single £1.50
Child Return £2.00   Child Single £1.50

Detailed Directions by Car:
Nene Park is situated on the A605 Oundle Road. Follow the brown tourist signs for Nene Park.

FFESTINIOG RAILWAY

Address: Ffestiniog Railway, Harbour Station, Porthmadog, Gwynedd LL49 9NF	**Nº of Steam Locos:** 12
Telephone Nº: (01766) 516000	**Nº of Other Locos:** 12
Year Formed: 1832	**Nº of Members:** 5,000
Location of Line: Porthmadog to Blaenau Ffestiniog	**Annual Membership Fee:** £26.00
	Approx Nº of Visitors P.A.: 360,000
Length of Line: 13½ miles	**Gauge:** 1 foot 11½ inches
	Web Site: www.festrail.co.uk

GENERAL INFORMATION

Nearest Mainline Station: Blaenau Ffestiniog (interchange) or Minffordd
Nearest Bus Station: Bus stop next to stations at Porthmadog & Blaenau Ffestiniog
Car Parking: Parking available at Porthmadog, Blaenau Ffestiniog, Minffordd and Tan-y-Bwlch
Coach Parking: Available at Porthmadog and Blaenau Ffestiniog
Souvenir Shop(s): Yes **Food & Drinks:** Yes

SPECIAL INFORMATION

The Railway runs through the spectacular scenery of Snowdonia National Park and the line now links up with the Welsh Highland Railway.

OPERATING INFORMATION

Opening Times: 2015 dates: Daily service from 24th March to 1st November. A limited service operates in the Winter and Santa Specials run on December dates. Please contact the railway for further details.
Steam Working: Most trains are steam hauled.
Prices: Adult £21.50 (Round-trip return ticket)
  Concessions £19.40 (Round-trip return)
One child travels free with each adult (or concession fare), additional children travel for half the fare.
Reductions are available groups of 20 or more.
Cheaper fares are also available for single rides and shorter journeys.

E-mail: enquiries@festrail.co.uk

Detailed Directions by Car:
Portmadog is easily accessible from the Midlands – take the M54/A5 to Corwen then the A494 to Bala onto the A4212 to Trawsfynydd and the A470 (becomes the A487 from Maentwrog) to Porthmadog. From Chester take the A55 to Llandudno Junction and the A470 to Blaenau Ffestiniog. Both Stations are well-signposted.

GARTELL LIGHT RAILWAY

Address: Common Lane, Yenston,
Templecombe, Somerset BA8 0NB
Telephone N°: (01963) 370752
Year Formed: 1991
Location of Line: South of Templecombe
Length of Line: ¾ mile

N° of Steam Locos: 2
N° of Other Locos: 3
Approx N° of Visitors P.A.: 3,000
Gauge: 2 feet
Web site: www.glr-online.co.uk

GENERAL INFORMATION

Nearest Mainline Station: Templecombe (1¼ miles)
Nearest Bus Station: Wincanton
Car Parking: Free parking adjacent to the station
Coach Parking: Adjacent to the station
Souvenir Shop(s): Yes
Food & Drinks: Meals, snacks and drinks available

SPECIAL INFORMATION

Part of the line runs along the track bed of the old
Somerset & Dorset Joint Railway. The line has
recently been extended and now features a working
junction, flyover, road crossing and a new northern
terminus

OPERATING INFORMATION

Opening Times: 2015 dates: 6th April; 4th May;
25th May; 27th & 28th June (Steam & Vintage show)
26th July; 30th & 31st August; 27th September and
25th October. Trains depart at frequent intervals
between 10.30am and 4.30pm.
Steam Working: Every operating day.
Prices: Adult £7.50
            Senior Citizen £6.00
            Child £4.00
            Family £20.00 (2 adults + 3 children)
Note: Tickets permit unlimited travel by any train
on the day of purchase. Under-5s travel for free.

Detailed Directions by Car:
From All Parts: The Railway is situated off the A357 just south of Templecombe and on open days is clearly
indicated by the usual brown tourist signs.

GIANT'S CAUSEWAY & BUSHMILLS RAILWAY

Address: Giant's Causeway Station, Runkerry Road, Bushmills, Co. Antrim, Northern Ireland BT57 8SZ	**Nº of Steam Locos:** 2
	Nº of Other Locos: 2
	Nº of Members: None
Telephone Nº: (028) 2073-2844	**Approx Nº of Visitors P.A.:** 50,000
Year Formed: 2002	**Gauge:** 3 feet
Location: Between the distillery village of Bushmills and the Giant's Causeway	**Web site:**
	www.freewebs.com/giantscausewayrailway
Length of Line: 2 miles	

GENERAL INFORMATION

Nearest Northern Ireland Railway Station: Coleraine/Portrush

Nearest Bus Station: Coleraine/Portrush

Car Parking: Car Park fee at Giant's Causeway Station is refunded upon ticket purchase. By parking at the Bushmills Station and taking the railway expensive parking charges at the Causeway itself can be avoided.

Coach Parking: Available on site

Souvenir Shop(s): Yes

Food & Drinks: At Giant's Causeway Station only

SPECIAL INFORMATION

The railway links the distillery village of Bushmills (open to visitors) to the World Heritage Site of the Giant's Causeway. The railway itself is built on the final two miles of the pioneering hydro-electric tramway which linked the Giant's Causeway to the main railway at Portrush from 1883 to 1949.

OPERATING INFORMATION

Opening Times: Daily in July and August, over St. Patrick's Day weekend and for Easter week. Also open at weekends from Easter to the end of June and in October & September. Trains run from 11.00am.

Steam Working: Please contact the railway for further information.

Prices: Adult Return £5.00
              Child Return £3.00

Note: Group rates are also available.

Detailed Directions by Car:
From Belfast take the M2 to the junction with the A26 (for Antrim, Ballymena and Coleraine). Follow the A26/M2/A26. From Ballymoney onwards Bushmills and the Giant's Causeway are well signposted. The railway is also well signposted in the immediate vicinity.

GOLDEN VALLEY LIGHT RAILWAY

Address: Butterley Station, Ripley, Derbyshire DE5 3QZ	**Nº of Steam Locos**: 2
Telephone Nº: (01773) 747674	**Nº of Other Locos**: 19
Year Formed: 1987	**Nº of Members**: 75
Location of Line: Butterley, near Ripley	**Annual Membership Fee**: £16.00
Length of Line: Four-fifths of a mile	**Approx Nº of Visitors P.A.**: 10,000
	Gauge: 2 feet
	Web site: www.gvlr.org.uk

GENERAL INFORMATION

Nearest Mainline Station: Alfreton (6 miles)
Nearest Bus Station: Bus stop outside the Station
Car Parking: Free parking at site – ample space
Coach Parking: Free parking at site
Souvenir Shop(s): Yes – at Butterley and Swanwick
Food & Drinks: Yes – both sites

SPECIAL INFORMATION

The Golden Valley Light Railway is part of the Midland Railway – Butterley and runs from the museum site through the country park to Newlands Inn Station close to the Cromford Canal and the pub of the same name.

OPERATING INFORMATION

Opening Times: 2015 dates: Weekends and Bank Holidays from 1st April to 1st November and Wednesdays to Sundays during the School Holidays. Trains run from 11.45am to 4.15pm.
Steam Working: One weekend per month – please contact the railway for further details.
Prices: Adult £2.00
Children £1.00

Detailed Directions by Car:
From All Parts: From the M1 exit at Junction 28 and take the A38 towards Derby. The Centre is signposted at the junction with the B6179.

GREAT LAXEY MINE RAILWAY

Address: Laxey Valley Gardens, Laxey, Isle of Man	**Nº of Steam Locos:** 2
	Nº of Other Locos: 1
Telephone Nº: (01624) 861706 (Secretary)	**Nº of Members:** Approximately 300
Year Formed: 2004	**Annual Membership Fee:** £10.00
Location of Line: Laxey Valley Gardens	**Approx Nº of Visitors P.A.:** 7,000
Length of Line: 550 yards	**Gauge:** 19 inches
	Web site: www.laxeyminerailway.im

GENERAL INFORMATION

Nearest Mainline Station: Laxey, Manx Electric Railway
Nearest Bus Station: Laxey
Car Parking: Available nearby
Coach Parking: Available nearby
Souvenir Shop(s): Yes
Food & Drinks: There are a number of Cafes nearby

SPECIAL INFORMATION

The Great Laxey Mine Railway is the recently restored surface section of the former mine tramway, the first section of which was opened in 1823. Originally worked by ponies, these were replaced by two steam locomotives in 1877. These engines were scrapped in 1935 but the restored line now uses two working replicas. A few minutes walk from the terminus of the railway is the Lady Isabella water wheel, the largest in the world. The railway itself is operated entirely by volunteers.

OPERATING INFORMATION

Opening Times: 2015 dates: Every Saturday and Bank Holiday from Easter until the end of September. A number of Special Event Days are operated throughout the season, details of which are advertised on the railway's web site.
Trains run from 11.00am to 4.30pm.
Steam Working: All trains are steam-hauled
Prices: Adult Return £2.00
Child Return £1.00 (Under-5s ride free)

Detailed Directions by Car:
Laxey is situated approximately 8 miles to the north east of Douglas on the A2 coast road.

GREAT WHIPSNADE RAILWAY

Address: ZSL Whipsnade Zoo, Dunstable LU6 2LF **Telephone Nº**: (01582) 872171 **Year Formed**: 1970 **Location of Line**: ZSL Whipsnade Zoo, Near Dunstable **Length of Line**: 1¾ miles	**Nº of Steam Locos**: 2 **Nº of Other Locos**: 5 **Nº of Members**: None **Approx Nº of Visitors P.A.**: 130,000 **Gauge**: 2 feet 6 inches **Web site**: www.zsl.org

GENERAL INFORMATION

Nearest Mainline Station: Luton (7 miles)
Nearest Bus Station: Dunstable (3 miles)
Car Parking: Available just outside the park
Coach Parking: Available just outside the park
Souvenir Shop(s): Next to the Station
Food & Drinks: Available

SPECIAL INFORMATION

The Railway is situated in the ZSL Whipsnade Zoo operated by the Zoological Society of London.

OPERATING INFORMATION

Opening Times: The zoo is open daily from 10.00am throughout the year. Closing time varies from 4.00pm to 6.00pm depending on the time of the year. The railway runs daily from the Easter Holidays until the end of October half-term and at weekends at some other times of the year. Contact the zoo for further details.
Steam Working: Every operating day.
Prices: Adult £25.00
        Child £18.00 (Ages 3 to 15 years)
        Senior Citizen £22.50
Note: The above prices are for entrance into the Zoo itself and include a voluntary donation.
Train rides are an additional charge:
Adults £4.50 Children £1.50 Concessions £3.50

Detailed Directions by Car:
From All Parts: Exit the M1 at Junction 11 and take the A505 then the B489. Follow signs for Whipsnade Zoo.

GROUDLE GLEN RAILWAY

Address: Groudle Glen, Onchan, Isle of Man	**Nº of Steam Locos:** 2
Telephone Nº: (01624) 670453 (weekends)	**Nº of Other Locos:** 3
Year Formed: 1982 **Re-Opened:** 1986	**Nº of Members:** 600
Location of Line: Groudle Glen	**Annual Membership Fee:** £12.00 (Adult)
Length of Line: ¾ mile	**Approx Nº of Visitors P.A.:** 10,000
Gauge: 2 feet	**Correspondence:** 29 Hawarden Avenue, Douglas, Isle of Man IM1 4BP
	Web site: www.ggr.org.uk

GENERAL INFORMATION

Nearest Mainline Station: Manx Electric Railway
Nearest Bus Station: Douglas Bus Station
Car Parking: At the entrance to the Glen
Coach Parking: At the entrance to the Glen
Souvenir Shop(s): Yes
Food & Drinks: Coffee and Tea available

SPECIAL INFORMATION

The Railway runs through a picturesque glen to a coastal headland where there are the remains of a Victorian Zoo. The Railway was built in 1896 and closed in 1962.

OPERATING INFORMATION

Opening Times: 2015 dates: Easter Sunday and Monday then Sundays from 3rd May to 27th September 11.00am to 4.30pm. Also most Wednesday evenings from 17th June to 26th August – 7.00pm to 9.00pm.
Steam Working: Contact the Railway for details.
Prices: Adult Return £4.00
Child Return £2.00
Note: Joint fares are also available to include a Manx Electric Railway journey from Derby Castle.

Detailed Directions by Car:
The Railway is situated on the coast road to the north of Douglas.

HALL LEYS MINIATURE RAILWAY

Address: Hall Leys Park, Matlock, Derbyshire
Telephone Nº: 07525 217116
Year Formed: 1948
Location of Line: Hall Leys Park
Length of Line: 200 yards

Nº of Steam Locos: None
Nº of Other Locos: 1
Approx Nº of Visitors P.A.: Not known
Gauge: 9½ inches

GENERAL INFORMATION

Nearest Mainline Station: Matlock (½ mile)
Nearest Bus Station: Matlock (by the train station)
Car Parking: Available near the train station on the new bypass
Coach Parking: As above

SPECIAL INFORMATION

The Hall Leys Miniature Railway has operated in Matlock since 1948 and is one of only 4 railways in the country to run a line with the unusual 9½ inch gauge. The park hosts a number of other attractions including a children's playground with a paddling pool, a lake with motor boats, a skate park and bowling and putting greens.

OPERATING INFORMATION

Opening Times: Weekends from mid-March to the end of September and daily during the school holidays in this period.
Steam Working: None at present.
Prices: 70p per ride.

Detailed Directions by Car:
Hall Leys Park is situated in the centre of Matlock between the River Derwent and the A615 Causeway Lane.

HASTINGS MINIATURE RAILWAY

Address: Rock-a-Nore Station, Old Town, Hastings TN34 3DW
Telephone Nº: 07773 645228
Year Formed: 1948
Location: Between Hastings Old Town and the Historic Fishing Beach & Museum
Length of Line: 680 yards

Nº of Steam Locos: None
Nº of Other Locos: 7
Approx Nº of Visitors P.A.: 20,000
Gauge: 10¼ inches
Web: www.hastingsminiaturerailway.co.uk

GENERAL INFORMATION

Nearest Mainline Station: Hastings (1 mile)
Car Parking: Limited parking available nearby
Coach Parking: None
Souvenir Shop(s): Yes
Food & Drinks: Available nearby

SPECIAL INFORMATION

The Hastings Miniature Railway, which opened on 5th June 1948, runs along the sea front area of Hastings Old Town and is a popular attraction.

OPERATING INFORMATION

Opening Times: Weekends throughout the year from 11.00am to 5.00pm (12.00pm to 4.00pm during the winter months) and also daily during through the School Holidays and during the Autumn half-term holidays.
Steam Working: None – steam profile engines only.
Prices: Adult Return £3.00
Child Return £3.00
Adult Day Rover £7.00
Child Day Rover £5.50
Family Day Rover £22.00
(2 Adults + 2 Children)

Detailed Directions by Car:
The Railway is located to the eastern (Fisherman's End) of Hastings Old Town, just off the A259 and next to the Hastings Fishing Museum.

Hayling Seaside Railway

Address: Beachlands, Sea Front Road, Hayling Island, Hampshire PO11 0AG	**Nº of Steam Locos**: Visiting locos only
Telephone Nº: 07775 696912	**Nº of Other Locos**: 4
Year Formed: 2001	**Nº of Members**: Approximately 100
Location: Beachlands to Eastoke Corner	**Annual Membership Fee**: £10.00
Length of Line: 1 mile	**Approx Nº of Visitors P.A.**: 25,000
Web site: www.haylingseasiderailway.com	**Gauge**: 2 feet
	E-mail: contact@haylingseasiderailway.com

GENERAL INFORMATION

Nearest Mainline Station: Havant
Nearest Bus Station: Beachlands
Car Parking: Spaces are available at both Beachlands and Eastoke Corner.
Coach Parking: Beachlands and Eastoke Corner
Souvenir Shop(s): Yes
Food & Drinks: Available

SPECIAL INFORMATION

The Railway runs along Hayling Island beach front where there are fantastic views across the Solent to the Isle of Wight.

OPERATING INFORMATION

Opening Times: Every Saturday, Sunday and Wednesday throughout the year and daily during the School holidays. Various specials run at different times of the year – please check the web site or phone the Railway for further details. The first train normally departs at 11.00am from Beachlands (from 10.00am on Wednesdays).

Steam Working: Visiting locos only. Please contact the railway for further information.

Prices: Adult Return £4.00
              Child/Senior Citizen Return £3.00
              Family Return £9.00 (2 Adult + 2 Child)
              Well-behaved Dogs 50p!

Detailed Directions by Car:
Exit the A27 at Havant Roundabout and proceed to Hayling Island and Beachlands Station following the road signs to Beachlands. Parking is available south of the Carousel Amusement Park. Beachlands Station is within the car park.

HEATHERSLAW LIGHT RAILWAY

Address: Ford Forge, Heatherslaw, Cornhill-on-Tweed TD12 4TJ
Telephone Nº: (01890) 820244
Year Formed: 1989
Location of Line: Ford & Etal Estates between Wooler & Berwick
Length of Line: Almost 2½ miles

Nº of Steam Locos: 1
Nº of Other Locos: 2
Approx Nº of Visitors P.A.: 30,000
Gauge: 15 inches
Website: www.heatherslawlightrailway.co.uk
E-mail: info@heatherslawlightrailway.co.uk

GENERAL INFORMATION

Nearest Mainline Station: Berwick-upon-Tweed (10 miles)
Nearest Bus Station: Berwick-upon-Tweed (10 mls)
Car Parking: Available on site
Coach Parking: Available on site
Souvenir Shop(s): Yes
Food & Drinks: Available

SPECIAL INFORMATION

The railway runs from Heatherslaw to Etel Castle along the banks of the River Till. A choice of semi-open and fully enclosed coaches are available to passengers, even on the wettest of days!

OPERATING INFORMATION

Opening Times: 2015 dates: Daily from 29th March to 1st November. Trains run hourly from 11.00am to 3.00pm (until 4.00pm in July & August)
Steam Working: Daily except when maintenance is is being carried out on the engine.
Prices: Adult Return £6.50
 Child Return £4.50 (Under 5's: £2.50)
 Senior Citizen Return £6.00

Detailed Directions by Car:
From the North: Take the A697 from Coldstream and the railway is about 5 miles along.
From the South: Take the A697 from Wooler and Millfield.

ISLE OF MAN STEAM RAILWAY

Address: Isle of Man Railways, Banks Circus, Douglas, Isle of Man   IM1 5PT
Telephone Nº: (01624) 662525
Year Formed: 1873
Location of Line: Douglas to Port Erin
Length of Line: 15½ miles

Nº of Steam Locos: 7
Nº of Other Locos: 2
Approx Nº of Visitors P.A.: 140,000
Gauge: 3 feet
Web site: www.iombusandrail.info

GENERAL INFORMATION

Nearest Mainline Station: Not applicable
Car Parking: Limited parking at all stations
Coach Parking: Available at Port Erin
Souvenir Shop(s): Souvenirs are available from all manned stations and from the shop at Port Erin Railway Museum
Food & Drinks: Yes – Douglas & Port Erin stations

SPECIAL INFORMATION

The Isle of Man Steam Railway is operated by the Isle of Man Government. A number of special events are held at the railway throughout the year.

OPERATING INFORMATION

Opening Times: 2015 Dates: Daily from 6th March to 8th November but closed on most Tuesdays and Wednesdays in March, September and October and most Wednesdays and Thursdays in April and May. Day and evening services are available during some of the summer months. Please contact the railway or check the web site for further details.
Steam Working: All scheduled services
Prices: Prices vary with 1, 3, 5 & 7 day Go Explore tickets also available which include travel on buses, the Snaefell and Manx Electric Railways and Douglas Corporation Horse Trams. Railcards and Season Tickets are also available.

Detailed Directions:
By Sea from Heysham (Lancashire) or Liverpool to reach Isle of Man. By Air from Belfast, Birmingham, Dublin, Glasgow, Gloucester, Jersey, Liverpool, Manchester, Newcastle, Bristol and London. Douglas Station is ½ mile inland from the Sea Terminal at the end of North Quay.

KERR'S MINIATURE RAILWAY

Address: West Links Park, Arbroath, Tayside, Scotland	**Nº of Steam Locos:** 2
	Nº of Other Locos: 4
Telephone Nº: (01241) 874074 or 879249	**Approx Nº of Visitors P.A.:** 10,000
Year Formed: 1935	**Gauge:** 10¼ inches
Location: Seafront, West Links Park	**Website:** www.kerrsminiaturerailway.co.uk
Length of Line: 400 yards	**E-mail:** info@kerrsminiaturerailway.co.uk

GENERAL INFORMATION

Nearest Mainline Station: Arbroath (1½ miles)
Nearest Bus Station: Arbroath (1½ miles)
Car Parking: Available 600 yards from railway
Coach Parking: Available 600 yards from railway
Souvenir Shop(s): Gifts available
Food & Drinks: Cafe stall in West Links Park

SPECIAL INFORMATION

The Railway is Scotland's oldest passenger-carrying miniature railway. It is a family-run enterprise not run for profit which is staffed by volunteers. The track itself runs alongside the Dundee to Aberdeen mainline.

OPERATING INFORMATION

Opening Times: 2015 dates: Daily during the Easter Holidays then weekends from 28th March to the end of September. Open daily from 27th June to 30th August.
Opening times are 11.00am to 4.00pm.
Steam Working: No set pattern but Steam is more likely to be running on Sundays than other dates.
Prices: Adults £1.50
Children £1.00

Detailed Directions by Car:
From All Parts: West Links Park is a seaside location which runs parallel to the A92 Coastal Tourist Route in Arbroath. Turn off the A92 at the West Links Park/KMR sign. The railway is then 600 yards due West along the seafront.

KIRKLEES LIGHT RAILWAY

Address: Park Mill Way, Clayton West, near Huddersfield, W. Yorks. HD8 9XJ
Telephone Nº: (01484) 865727
Year Formed: 1991
Location of Line: Clayton West to Shelley
Length of Line: 4 miles

Nº of Steam Locos: 4
Nº of Other Locos: 2
Approx Nº of Visitors P.A.: 48,000
Gauge: 15 inches
Web site: www.kirkleeslightrailway.com

Photograph courtesy of Karen Ashton

GENERAL INFORMATION

Nearest Mainline Station: Denby Dale (4 miles)
Nearest Bus Station: Bus stops at the bottom of Park Mill Way. Take the 435 and 436 from Wakefield or the 80 and 81 from Huddersfield.
Car Parking: Ample free parking at site
Coach Parking: Ample free parking at site
Souvenir Shop(s): Yes
Food & Drinks: Yes

SPECIAL INFORMATION

The Railway now has outdoor play areas for children, a 7¼ inch railway at Clayton West and Shelley Tearooms open during railway operations.

OPERATING INFORMATION

Opening Times: 2015 dates: Every weekend and Bank Holiday throughout the year and daily during school holidays. Open Wednesday to Sunday from 3rd June to 19th July to 2nd September.
Steam Working: All trains are steam-hauled (subject to availability). Train timetables vary, so please check the website for further information.
Prices: Adults £7.50
　　　　　Children (3-16 years) £5.50
　　　　　Children (under 3 years) Free of charge
　　　　　Concessions £6.50
　　　　　Family Ticket £24.00
Note: Prices at Special events may vary.

Detailed Directions by Car:
The Railway is located on the A636 Wakefield to Denby Dale road. Turn off the M1 at Junction 39 and follow the A636 signposted for Denby Dale. Continue for approximately 4 miles then the railway is on the left after passing under the railway bridge and is situated at the top of the Industrial Estate, just before the village of Scissett.

LAKESHORE RAILROAD

Address: 6 Marina Drive, South Shields, NE33 2NH	**No of Steam Locos:** 2
	No of Other Locos: 1
Telephone No: 07745 350983	**Approx No of Visitors P.A.:** 65,000
Year Formed: 1972	**Gauge:** 9½ inches
Length of Line: 570 yards	**Web site:** www.lakeshorerailroad.co.uk
	E-mail: info@lakeshorerailroad.co.uk

GENERAL INFORMATION

Nearest Mainline Station: South Shields (¾ mile)
Nearest Bus Station: Newcastle (11 miles)
Car Parking: Available on the seafront
Coach Parking: Available nearby
Souvenir Shop(s): None
Food & Drinks: Available nearby

SPECIAL INFORMATION

The Lakeshore Railroad runs two American-designed locomotives – hence the name!

OPERATING INFORMATION

Opening Times: Weekends throughout the year and daily from mid-May to mid-September and during other School Holidays except for Christmas. Trains run from 11.00am to 5.00pm.
Steam Working: Daily, subject to availability
Prices: Adults £1.20
Children £1.20 (Free for Under-3s)

Detailed Directions by Car:
From All Parts: Take the A194 into South Shields. The railway is located by the Seafront in South Marine Park and can be found by following the brown tourist signs marked for the 'Seafront'.

LAPPA VALLEY STEAM RAILWAY

Address: St. Newlyn East, Newquay, Cornwall   TR8 5LX
Telephone Nº: (01872) 510317
Year Formed: 1974
Location of Line: Benny Halt to East Wheal Rose, near St. Newlyn East
Length of Line: 1 mile

Nº of Steam Locos: 2
Nº of Other Locos: 2
Approx Nº of Visitors P.A.: 50,000
Gauge: 15 inches
Web site: www.lappavalley.co.uk

GENERAL INFORMATION

Nearest Mainline Station:
Newquay (5 miles)
Nearest Bus Station: Newquay (5 miles)
Car Parking: Free parking at Benny Halt
Coach Parking: Free parking is available at Benny Halt
Souvenir Shop(s): Yes
Food & Drinks: Yes

SPECIAL INFORMATION

The railway runs on part of the former Newquay to Chacewater branch line. Site also has a Grade II listed mine building, boating, play areas for children and 2 other miniature train rides.

OPERATING INFORMATION

Opening Times: 2015 dates: Daily from 28th March to 1st November.
Steam Working: 10.30am to 4.30pm during the summer months.
Prices: Adult £12.00
        Child £9.50
        Family £37.00
              (2 adults + 2 children)
        Family £40.00
              (2 adults + 3 children)
        Senior Citizen £10.00

Detailed Directions by Car:
The railway is signposted from the A30 at the Summercourt-Mitchell bypass, from the A3075 south of Newquay and the A3058 east of Newquay.

LAUNCESTON STEAM RAILWAY

Address: The Old Gasworks, St. Thomas Road, Launceston, Cornwall   PL15 8DA
Telephone Nº: (01566) 775665
Year Formed: Opened in 1983
Location of Line: Launceston to Newmills
Length of Line: 2½ miles

Nº of Steam Locos: 4
Nº of Other Locos: 4
Gauge: 1 foot 11 $\frac{5}{8}$ inches
Web site: www.launcestonsr.co.uk

GENERAL INFORMATION

Nearest Mainline Station: Liskeard (15 miles)
Nearest Bus Station: Launceston (½ mile)
Car Parking: At Station, Newport Industrial Estate, Launceston
Coach Parking: As above
Souvenir Shop(s): Yes – also with a bookshop
Food & Drinks: Cafe serving hot and cold meals

SPECIAL INFORMATION

The Launceston Steam Railway runs for two and a half miles through the glorious Kensey Valley along the trackbed of the old North Cornwall Railway, where once express trains from Waterloo passed.

OPERATING INFORMATION

Opening Times: 2015 dates: 5th to 10th April; 17th to 31st May (but closed on 23rd & 30th May). Sundays, Mondays and Tuesdays in June. Daily from 1st July until the 25th September but closed on Saturdays. Also open daily from 25th to 30th October.
Steam Working: Hourly from 11.00am to 4.00pm.
Prices: Adult £10.00
　　　　　Child £6.50
　　　　　Family £29.00 (2 adults + 4 children)
　　　　　Senior Citizen £8.75
Group rates are available upon application.

Detailed Directions by Car:
From the East/West: Drive to Launceston via the A30 and look for the brown Steam Engine Tourist signs. Use the L.S.R. car park at the Newport Industrial Estate; From Bude/Holsworthy: Take the A388 to Launceston and follow signs for the town centre. After the river bridge turn left at the traffic lights into Newport Industrial Estate and use the L.S.R. car park. Sat Navs use the following post code: PL15 8EX.

LEADHILLS & WANLOCKHEAD RAILWAY

Address: The Station, Leadhills,
Lanarkshire ML12 6XP
Telephone Nº: None
Year Formed: 1983
Location of Line: Leadhills, Lanarkshire
Length of Line: ¾ mile (at present)

Nº of Steam Locos: 1 (Not in operation)
Nº of Other Locos: 5
Nº of Members: Approximately 100
Annual Membership Fee: Adult £15.00
Approx Nº of Visitors P.A.: 3,000
Gauge: 2 feet
Web site: www.leadhillsrailway.co.uk

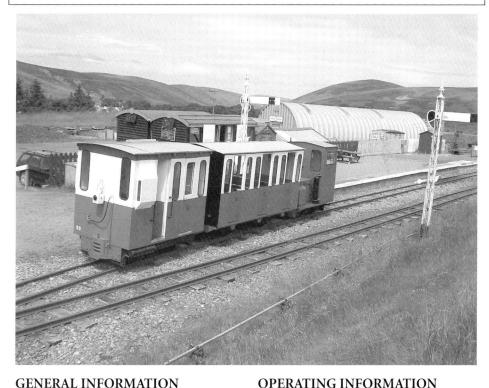

GENERAL INFORMATION

Nearest Mainline Station: Sanquhar
Nearest Bus Station: Lanark and Sanquhar
Car Parking: Available on site
Coach Parking: Available on site
Souvenir Shop(s): Yes
Food & Drinks: Yes

SPECIAL INFORMATION

Leadhills & Wanlockhead Railway is the highest
adhesion railway in the UK with the summit 1,498
feet above sea level.

OPERATING INFORMATION

Opening Times: Weekends from Easter until the
end of September. There are also a number of
'Special Events' during the year. Please contact the
railway for further information about these. Trains
run from 11.20am to 4.20pm on operating days.
Steam Working: None at present
Prices: Adult Day Ticket £4.00
Child Day Ticket £2.00
Family Day Ticket £10.00
　　　(2 adults and up to 2 children)
Concession Day Ticket £3.00

Detailed Directions by Car:
From the South: Exit the M74 at Junction 14 and follow the A702 to Elvanfoot. Turn right onto the B7040 and
follow to Leadhills. Turn left at the T-junction and Station Road is a short distance on the left; From the North: Exit
the M74 at Junction 13 for Abington and follow signs for Leadhills along the B797. Station Road is on the left
shortly after entering Leadhills.

LEEDS INDUSTRIAL MUSEUM

Address: Canal Road, Armley, Leeds, LS12 2QF
Telephone Nº: (0113) 378-3173
Year Formed: 1985
Location of Line: Armley Mills, Leeds
Length of Line: ¼ mile

Nº of Steam Locos: 8 (One in steam)
Nº of Other Locos: 31 (One operational)
Approx Nº of Visitors P.A.: 42,000
Gauges: 2 feet and 18 inches
Web site: www.leeds.gov.uk/ArmleyMills

GENERAL INFORMATION

Nearest Mainline Station: Leeds City (2 miles)
Nearest Bus Station: Leeds (2 miles)
Car Parking: Available on site
Coach Parking: Available
Souvenir Shop(s): Yes
Food & Drinks: Tea and coffee only

SPECIAL INFORMATION

A number of Leeds-built locomotives are on display at the museum in addition to a variety of static engines and machinery.

OPERATING INFORMATION

Opening Times: Closed on Mondays but otherwise, daily throughout the year. Open on Bank Holiday Mondays, however. Open from 10.00am to 5.00pm (but from 1.00pm to 5.00pm on Sundays).
Steam Working: Bank Holiday Sundays and Mondays and one some other Special Event days. Please contact the museum for further details.
Prices: Adults £3.30
      Children £1.20
      Concessions £1.70
      Family Ticket £6.50
Lower prices are charged to "Leeds Card" holders.
Note: The line is used for demonstrations only – unfortunately, rides are not available.

Detailed Directions by Car:
From All Parts: The Museum is located next to the Cardigan Field Leisure Complex which is just to the South of the A65 Kirkstall Road.

LEIGHTON BUZZARD RAILWAY

Address: Pages Park Station, Billington Road, Leighton Buzzard, Beds. LU7 4TN	**Nº of Steam Locos**: 14
	Nº of Other Locos: 53
Telephone Nº: (01525) 373888	**Nº of Members**: 400
E-mail: info@buzzrail.co.uk	**Annual Membership Fee**: £24.00
Year Formed: 1967	**Approx Nº of Visitors P.A.**: 20,000
Location of Line: Leighton Buzzard	**Gauge**: 2 feet
Length of Line: 3 miles	**Web site**: www.buzzrail.co.uk

GENERAL INFORMATION

Nearest Mainline Station: Leighton Buzzard (2 miles)
Nearest Bus Station: Leighton Buzzard (¾ mile)
Car Parking: Free parking adjacent
Coach Parking: Free parking adjacent
Souvenir Shop(s): Yes   **Food & Drinks**: Yes

SPECIAL INFORMATION

The railway was constructed in 1919 to carry sand from local quarries using surplus materials from World War I battlefield supply lines. Now a working museum, it transports passengers and is operated by volunteers.

OPERATING INFORMATION

Opening Times: 2015 dates: Sundays from 15th March to 22nd October plus Bank Holiday weekends. Also open on some Saturdays and weekdays. Trains run from 10.40am to 3.40pm and Christmas and New Year services run on some dates in December. Please visit the railway's web site for further details.
Steam Working: Most operating days.
Prices: Adult £9.50
Child £5.50
Senior Citizens £8.00
Note: A variety of Family Tickets, Day Rover tickets and Single tickets are also available. The prices shown above include an optional Gift Aid donation.

Detailed Directions by Car:
Travel to Leighton Buzzard then follow the brown tourist signs showing a steam train. Pages Park Station is ¾ mile to the south of the Town Centre. From the A505/A4146 bypass, turn towards Leighton Buzzard at the roundabout following the 'Narrow Gauge Railway' brown tourist signs.

LINCOLNSHIRE COAST LIGHT RAILWAY

Address: Skegness Water Leisure Park, Walls Lane, Skegness PE25 1JF
Telephone Nº: (01754) 897400
E-mail: johnchappell@ricsonline.org
Year Formed: 1960 (re-opened in 2009)
Location of Line: Skegness
Length of Line: ¾ miles

Nº of Steam Locos: 1 awaiting restoration
Nº of Other Locos: 4
Nº of Members: Approximately 50
Approx Nº of Visitors P.A.: 5,000
Gauge: 2 feet
Web site:
www.lincolnshire-coast-light-railway.co.uk

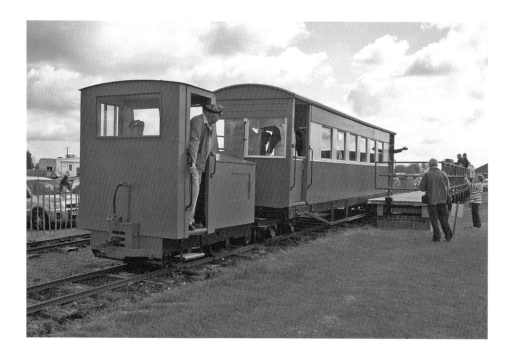

GENERAL INFORMATION

Nearest Mainline Station: Skegness (3 miles)
Nearest Bus Station: Skegness (3 miles)
Car Parking: Free parking available on site
Coach Parking: Free parking available on site
Souvenir Shop(s): None
Food & Drinks: Available

SPECIAL INFORMATION

The railway was originally located some distance up the coast at the Cleethorpes/Humberston 'Fitties' before closure during the 1980s.

OPERATING INFORMATION

Opening Times: 2015 dates: 2nd, 23rd & 24th May; 25th July; 1st, 8th, 15th, 22nd and 29th August. A special Gala Day will be held on 25th July when our historic First World War trench railway vehicles will be demonstrated with guided tours of our collection available. Other opening dates will be detailed on the railway's facebook page.
Steam Working: None at present.
Prices: Adults £1.00
Children £1.00

Detailed Directions by Car:
From All Parts: Take the A52 North from Skegness (signposted for Ingoldmells) and continue for 3 miles. Turn left onto Walls Lane opposite the Butlins signposted for the Water Leisure Park. After ¼ mile turn left into the Park and follow the signs for the Railway.

LITTLEHAMPTON RAILWAY

<table>
<tr><td>Address: Mewsbrook Park,
Littlehampton   BN16 2LX</td><td>No of Steam Locos: 1 (from mid-2015)</td></tr>
</table>

Address: Mewsbrook Park,
Littlehampton   BN16 2LX
Telephone No: (01460) 221303
Information No: 07746 907817
Year Formed: 1948
Location of Line: Mewsbrook Park
Length of Line: ½ mile

No of Steam Locos: 1 (from mid-2015)
No of Other Locos: 1
No of Members: Approximately 50
Approx No of Visitors P.A.: 18,000
Gauge: 12¼ inches
Website: www.littlehamptonrailway.co.uk
E-mail: info@littlehamptonrailway.co.uk

GENERAL INFORMATION

Nearest Mainline Station: Littlehampton (1 mile)
Nearest Bus Station: Littlehampton
Car Parking: Available at the swimming pool, at East Green and along the Sea Wall.
Coach Parking: Available at the swimming pool
Souvenir Shop(s): During special event days only
Food & Drinks: Cafes are adjacent to both stations

SPECIAL INFORMATION

The Littlehampton Railway is the oldest 12¼ inch gauge railway in the UK and runs from Mewsbrook Park to Norfolk Gardens. The railway is surrounded by a variety of leisure attractions including a boating lake and a 9-hole golf course.

OPERATING INFORMATION

Opening Times: Weekends and School Holidays from early February to the end of October (weather permitting). Trains run daily from 12.00am to 4.00pm and from 10.00am to 5.00pm in July and August.
Steam Working: The railway hopes to have its own loco steaming from mid-2015. Please contact the railway for further information.
Prices: Adult Return   £3.00
              Child Return   £2.00
              Family Ticket Return   £10.00
Note: High fares apply for special event days.

Detailed Directions by Car:
From All Parts: Take the A27 Brighton to Portsmouth road and follow signs for Littlehampton. Upon entering Littlehampton, follow signs for the Swimming Pool/Sea Front and, when you reach the Beach Road (which runs along parallel to the sea), head east and park either at East Green or further along to the Swimming Pool.

LLANBERIS LAKE RAILWAY

Address: Gilfach Ddu, Llanberis,
Gwynedd   LL55 4TY
Telephone Nº: (01286) 870549
Year Formed: 1970
Location of Line: Just off the A4086
Caernarfon to Capel Curig road at Llanberis
Length of Line: 2½ miles

Nº of Steam Locos: 3
Nº of Other Locos: 4
Approx Nº of Visitors P.A.: 80,000
Gauge: 1 foot 11½ inches
Web site: www.lake-railway.co.uk

GENERAL INFORMATION

Nearest Mainline Station: Bangor (8 miles)
Nearest Bus Station: Caernarfon (6 miles) (there is
a bus stop by Llanberis Station)
Car Parking: £4.00 Council car park on site
Coach Parking: Ample free parking on site
Souvenir Shop(s): Yes
Food & Drinks: Yes

SPECIAL INFORMATION

Llanberis Lake Railway runs along part of the
trackbed of the Padarn Railway which transported
slates for export and closed in 1961.

OPERATING INFORMATION

Opening Times: 2015 dates: Open most days from
29th March to 31st October as well as some other
dates. Closed on some Saturdays in April, May and
September and most Fridays and Saturdays in
October. Please send for a free timetable or check
out the railway's web site where an online booking
feature is now available.
Steam Working: Every operating day.
Trains generally run from 11.00am to 4.00pm.
Prices: Adult £8.20   Child £4.50
            Concessions £7.20
            Family tickets from £20.00
A range of family discounts are available.
Note: The Welsh Slate Museum is situated adjacent
to the Railway.

Detailed Directions by Car:
The railway is situated just off the A4086 Caernarfon to Capel Curig road. Follow signs for Padarn Country Park.

LONDON MUSEUM OF WATER & STEAM

Address: Kew Bridge Steam Museum, Green Dragon Lane, Brentford   TW8 0EN
Telephone Nº: (020) 8568-4757
Year Formed: 1986
Location of Line: Greater London
Length of Line: Under 1 mile

Nº of Steam Locos: 1
Nº of Other Locos: 1
Nº of Members: 750
Annual Membership Fee: £25.00 (Adult)
Approx Nº of Visitors P.A.: 18,500
Gauge: 2 feet
Web site: www.waterandsteam.org.uk

GENERAL INFO

Nearest Mainline Station: Kew Bridge (3 minute walk)
Nearest Bus Station: Bus stop across the road – Services 65, 267 and 237
Car Parking: Spaces for 20 cars available on site
Coach Parking: Available on site – book in advance
Souvenir Shop(s): Yes
Food & Drinks: Cafe open daily 11.00am to 4.00pm

SPECIAL INFO

The Museum is a former Victorian Pumping Station with a collection of working Steam Pumping Engines. The Railway demonstrates typical water board use of Railways.

OPERATING INFO

Opening Times: Daily throughout the year except from 25th to 27th December. Open from 11.00am to 4.00pm.
Steam Working: The pumping engines are in steam every weekend throughout the year and the railway is in steam every weekend from Easter to New Year.
Prices: Adults £11.50
　　　　　　Under-16s £5.00
　　　　　　　　(Under-5s free of charge)
　　　　　　Senior Citizen £10.00
　　　　　　Family Ticket £28.00
　　　　　　　　(2 adults + 2 children)
　　　　　　Family Ticket £16.50
　　　　　　　　(1 adult + 2 children)
Note: Annual tickets cost just £3.00 more than the daily prices shown!

Detailed Directions by Car:
From All Parts: Exit the M4 at Junction 1 and follow the A4 to Chiswick Roundabout. Take the exit signposted for Kew Gardens & Brentford. Go straight on at the next two sets of traffic lights following A315 towards Brentford. After 2nd set of lights take the first right for the Museum. The Museum is next to the tall Victorian tower.

Lynton & Barnstaple Railway

Address: Woody Bay Station, Martinhoe Cross, Parracombe, Devon EX31 4RA	**Nº of Steam Locos:** 2
Telephone Nº: (01598) 763487	**Nº of Other Locos:** 3
E-mail: enquiries@lynton-rail.co.uk	**Nº of Members:** 2,200
Year Formed: 1993	**Annual Membership Fee:** £26.00
Location of Line: North Devon	**Approx Nº of Visitors P.A.:** 35,000
Length of Line: One mile	**Gauge:** 1 foot 11½ inches
	Web site: www.lynton-rail.co.uk

Photo courtesy of Trevor A. Garnham

GENERAL INFORMATION

Nearest Mainline Station: Barnstaple
Nearest Bus Station: Barnstaple
Car Parking: Available at Woody Bay Station
Coach Parking: Available by prior arrangement
Souvenir Shop(s): Yes – at Woody Bay Station
Food & Drinks: Available at Woody Bay Station

SPECIAL INFORMATION

Original Lynton & Barnstaple Railway carriages built in 1898 and 1903 are now operating a regular passenger service.

OPERATING INFORMATION

Opening Times: Open most days from Easter until early November and selected dates in December. Please check with the railway for exact dates. Trains run from 10.45am to 4.00pm.
Steam Working: Most trains are steam-hauled except on Mondays and Fridays outside of the school holidays or in the event of breakdown.
Prices: Adult Return £7.50
             Child Return £3.00 (Ages 5-14)
             Senior Citizen Return £6.00
             Family Ticket £18 (2 Adults + 3 Children)
Note: Upgrades to First Class are available for £3.00 per person.

Detailed Directions by Car:
From All Parts: Woody Bay Station is located alongside the A39 halfway between Lynton and Blackmoor Gate and one mile north-east of the village of Parracombe.

MARGAM PARK RAILWAY

Address: Margam Country Park, Port Talbot SA13 2TJ
Telephone Nº: (01639) 881635
Year Formed: 1976
Location of Line: Margam Country Park
Length of Line: Almost 1½ miles

Nº of Steam Locos: None
Nº of Other Locos: 1
Approx Nº of Visitors P.A.: 200,000 (to the Park itself)
Gauge: 2 feet
Web site: www.margamcountrypark.co.uk

GENERAL INFORMATION

Nearest Mainline Station: Port Talbot (3 miles)
Nearest Bus Station: Port Talbot (3 miles)
Car Parking: Available on site for a £3.50 charge
Coach Parking: Available
Souvenir Shop(s): Yes
Food & Drinks: Available

SPECIAL INFORMATION

Set in 1,000 acres of glorious parkland, Margam Country Park features an 18th Century Orangery, a Tudor-Gothic Victorian Mansion House and a 12th Century Chapter House.

OPERATING INFORMATION

Opening Times: 2015 dates: Daily from 3rd April to 31st August. Trains run from 10.00am to 4.15pm.
Steam Working: None at present
Prices: Adults £1.80
Children £1.00
Concessions £1.00
Family Ticket £4.60 (2 adults + 2 children)

Detailed Directions by Car:
From All Parts: Exit the M4 at Junction 38 and take the A48 towards Pyle following the brown tourist signs for Margam Country Park. The Park is situated on the left hand side of the road.

Moseley Industrial Narrow Gauge Tramway, Toy and Mining Museum

Address: Tumblydown Farm, Tolgus Mount, Redruth TR15 3TA
Telephone Nº: (01209) 211191
Alternative Telephone Nº: 07511 256677
Year Formed: 1969 (formed in the northwest, relocated to Cornwall in 2000)
Location: ½ mile north of Redruth

Length of Line: 600 yards
Nº of Steam Locos: 1 road locomotive
Nº of Other Locos: 16
Approx Nº of Visitors P.A.: 4,000
Gauge: 2 feet
Web site: www.moseleymuseum.co.uk

GENERAL INFORMATION

Nearest Mainline Station: Redruth (2 miles)
Nearest Bus Station: Redruth (2 miles)
Car Parking: Available on site
Coach Parking: Available by prior arrangement
Souvenir Shop(s): Yes
Food & Drinks: Available by prior arrangement

SPECIAL INFORMATION

Moseley Museum is operated by volunteers who maintain and restore the vehicles and displays. Other attractions at the museum include collections of vintage toys and meccano, curios and mining equipment. Home of the Murdoch Flyer.

OPERATING INFORMATION

Opening Times: Open throughout the year for group and individual visits by prior arrangement, plus a number of special public open days. Also open on all Monday and Thursday afternoons. Please contact the museum for further details before visiting.
Steam Working: Operational road locomotive, 'The Murdoch Flyer'.
Prices: Free of charge but voluntary donations are gratefully received!

Detailed Directions by Car:
From the A30, turn on to the old Redruth bypass (A3047). Follow the brown tourist signs for Trickys Lodge. Tumblydown Farm is on the right about 200 yards past Trickys Lodge.

NATIONAL COAL MINING MUSEUM FOR ENGLAND

Address: Caphouse Colliery, New Road, Overton, Wakefield WF4 4RH **Telephone N°**: (01924) 848806 **Year Formed**: 1988 **Location of Line**: West Yorkshire **Length of Line**: 500 yards	**N° of Steam Locos**: None in service **N° of Other Locos**: 2 **Approx N° of Visitors P.A.**: 110,000 (to the Museum) **Gauge**: 2 feet 6 inches **Web site**: www.ncm.org.uk

GENERAL INFORMATION

Nearest Mainline Station: Wakefield (5 miles)
Nearest Bus Station: Wakefield (5 miles)
Car Parking: Available on site
Coach Parking: Available
Souvenir Shop(s): Yes   **Food & Drinks**: Available

SPECIAL INFORMATION

The National Coal Mining Museum for England offers an unusual combination of exciting experiences. The highlight of any visit is the underground tour where experienced local miners guide parties around the underground workings. Each visitor is provided with a hat, belt and battery, so that the true atmosphere of working life underground is captured. Above ground there are genuine pit ponies, a train ride, machinery displays, steam winder, pithead baths and the 42-acre rural site with its nature trail and adventure playground to be enjoyed. In addition, a modern visitor centre has been built with multimedia audio-visual displays, galleries and exhibitions, a licensed cafe and well-stocked shop.

OPERATING INFORMATION

Opening Times: Daily throughout the year except for Christmas Day, Boxing Day and New Year's Day. Open from 10.00am to 5.00pm.
Steam Working: None
Prices: Admission to the Museum is free of charge. Return train rides are only available during the school holidays and some other selected dates. Rides £1.00 per person.

Detailed Directions by Car:
From All Parts: Take the M1 to Wakefield and follow the brown tourist signs for the National Coal Mining Museum which is at the side of the A642 in Overton.

NEWBY HALL MINIATURE RAILWAY

Address: Newby Hall & Gardens, near Ripon   HG4 5AE
Telephone Nº: 0845 450-4068
Year Formed: 1971
Location of Line: Newby Hall, Ripon
Length of Line: Approximately 1 mile

Nº of Steam Locos: 1
Nº of Other Locos: 2
Nº of Members: None
Approx Nº of Passengers P.A.: 60,000
Gauge: 10¼ inches
Web site: www.newbyhall.com

GENERAL INFORMATION

Nearest Mainline Station: Knaresborough (7 miles)
Nearest Bus Station: Ripon (3 miles)
Car Parking: Free parking available on site
Coach Parking: Available
Souvenir Shop(s): No specific railway souvenirs
Food & Drinks: Available

SPECIAL INFORMATION

The railway is located within the gardens of Newby Hall and the track runs alongside the scenic River Ure.

OPERATING INFORMATION

Opening Times: 2015 dates: Open daily from 1st April until 27th September from 11.00am to 5.30pm. Trains operate at regular intervals throughout the day.
Steam Working: Sundays and Bank Holidays.
Prices: Return Ticket £1.80
Note: The price above is for train rides only. Entrance to the House and Gardens is an additional charge which must be paid to gain entry to the grounds.

Detailed Directions by Car:
From All Parts: Exit the A1(M) at Junction 48 when travelling from the South or Junction 49 travelling from the North and follow the brown tourist signs for Newby Hall (passing under the A1(M)).

NORTH BAY MINIATURE RAILWAY

Address: Burniston Road, Scarborough, North Yorkshire YO12 6PF	**Nº of Steam Locos**: None
	Nº of Other Locos: 4
Telephone Nº: (01723) 368791	**Nº of Members**: None
Year Opened: 1931	**Approx Nº of Visitors P.A.**: 200,000
Location: Peasholm Park to Scalby Mills	**Gauge**: 20 inches
Length of Line: 1 mile	**Web site**: www.nbr.org.uk

GENERAL INFORMATION

Nearest Mainline Station: Scarborough
Nearest Bus Station: Scarborough
Car Parking: Adjacent to the railway
Coach Parking: Adjacent to the railway
Souvenir Shop(s): Yes
Food & Drinks: Glass House Cafe in Peasholm Park

SPECIAL INFORMATION

The North Bay Miniature Railway was opened in 1931 and operates between Northstead Manor and Scalby Mills for the Sea Life Centre.

OPERATING INFORMATION

Opening Times: 2015 dates: Daily from 28th March until 1st November then at weekends and local school holidays during the winter. Trains run at varying times from 10.30am onwards, depending on the time of the year.
Please phone (01723) 368791 or check the railway's web site for further details.
Steam Working: None
Prices: Adult Return £3.50 (Single £2.90)
Child Return £2.70 (Single £2.20)

E-mail: gm@nbr.org.uk

Detailed Directions by Car:
From All Parts: Take the A64, A165 or A170 to Scarborough and follow the signs for North Bay Leisure Park. The railway is situated just off the A165 opposite Peasholm Park. Alternatively, follow signs for the Sea Life Centre for Scalby Mills Station.

OLD KILN LIGHT RAILWAY

Address: Rural Life Centre, Reeds Road, Tilford, Farnham, Surrey GU10 2DL	**Nº of Steam Locos**: 2
Telephone Nº: (01252) 795571	**Nº of Other Locos**: 10
Year Formed: 1975	**Nº of Members**: 14
Location: 3 miles south of Farnham	**Annual Membership Fee**: £25.00
Length of Line: ¾ mile **Gauge**: 2 feet	**Approx Nº of Visitors P.A.**: 21,000
	Web site: www.oldkilnlightrailway.com

GENERAL INFORMATION

Nearest Mainline Station: Farnham (4 miles)
Nearest Bus Station: Farnham
Car Parking: Free parking available on site
Coach Parking: Free parking available on site
Souvenir Shop(s): Yes
Food & Drinks: Available

SPECIAL INFORMATION

The Railway is part of the Rural Life Centre at Tilford. The Centre contains the biggest country life collection in the South of England with a wide range of attractions. A line extension to ¾ mile has recently been opened.

OPERATING INFORMATION

Opening Times: 2015 dates: The Rural Life Centre is open Wednesday to Sunday and Bank Holidays from March to October, 10.00am to 5.00pm. Open Wednesdays and Sundays only during the winter from 11.00am to 4.00pm. Also open for Santa Specials in December. Please contact the railway for further information about all these events.
Steam Working: No steam working during 2015 as the locomotive is undergoing its 10 year overhaul.
Prices: Diesel-hauled rides £1.00

Detailed Directions by Car:
The Rural Life Centre is situated 3 miles south of Farnham. From Farnham take the A287 southwards before turning left at Millbridge crossroads into Reeds Road. The Centre is on the left after about ½ mile, just after the Frensham Garden Centre; From the A3: Turn off at the Hindhead crossroads and head north to Tilford. Pass through Tilford, cross the River Wey then turn left into Reeds Road. The Centre is on the right after ½ mile.

PERRYGROVE RAILWAY

Address: Perrygrove Railway, Coleford, Gloucestershire GL16 8QB	**Nº of Steam Locos**: 3
Telephone Nº: (01594) 834991	**Nº of Other Locos**: 3
Year Formed: 1996	**Nº of Members**: 20
Location of Line: ½ mile south of Coleford	**Approx Nº of Visitors P.A.**: 25,000
Length of Line: ¾ mile	**Gauge**: 15 inches
	Web site: www.perrygrove.co.uk

GENERAL INFORMATION

Nearest Mainline Station: Lydney (for Parkend)
Nearest Bus Station: Bus stops in Coleford
Car Parking: Free parking available on site
Coach Parking: Free parking on site
Souvenir Shop(s): Yes
Food & Drinks: Sandwiches & light refreshments are available

SPECIAL INFORMATION

Perrygrove is a unique railway with 4 stations, all with access to private woodland walks. Lots of picnic tables are available in the open and under cover. There is also an indoor village with secret passages, a play area and an exciting Treetop Adventure accessible to all.

OPERATING INFORMATION

Opening Times: Every weekends and Bank Holiday throughout the year and daily during the local school holidays. Santa Specials also run in December (pre-booking is essential for these). Please contact the railway for further details. Railway opens at 10.30am with the last train time depending on the time of year.
Steam Working: Most services are steam-hauled and driver experience courses are also available.
Prices: Please contact the railway for details.

Detailed Directions by Car:
From All Parts: Travel to Coleford, Gloucestershire. Upon reaching the vicinity of Coleford, the Perrygrove Railway is clearly signposted with brown tourist signs from all directions.   SATNAVs use this post code: GL16 8QB

RAVENGLASS & ESKDALE RAILWAY

Address: Ravenglass, Cumbria CA18 1SW	**Gauge:** 15 inches
Telephone Nº: (01229) 717171	**Nº of Steam Locos:** 6
Year Formed: 1875	**Nº of Other Locos:** 8
Location: The Lake District National Park	**Nº of Members:** None
Length of Line: 7 miles	**Approx Nº of Visitors P.A.:** 120,000
	Web site: www.ravenglass-railway.co.uk
	E-mail: steam@ravenglass-railway.co.uk

GENERAL INFORMATION

Nearest Mainline Station: Ravenglass (adjacent)
Nearest Bus Stop: Ravenglass
Car Parking: Available at both terminals
Coach Parking: At Ravenglass
Souvenir Shop(s): Yes
Food & Drinks: Yes

SPECIAL INFORMATION

From Ravenglass, the Lake District's only coastal village, the line runs through two lovely valleys to the foot of England's highest mountain. A new station and visitor centre featuring Fellbites eatery, Scafell Gift Shop and the Eskdale Meeting Room is now open at Dalegarth (Eskdale).

OPERATING INFORMATION

Opening Times: 2015 dates: The service runs daily from 14th March until the 1st November inclusive. Trains also run during most weekends in the Winter, daily during February half-term and Santa Specials operate on other dates in December.
Open from 9.00am to 5.00pm (sometimes later during high season).
Steam Working: Most services are steam hauled.
Prices: Adult £13.20
      Child £6.60 (Ages 5 to 15)
      Under-5s travel free
      Family Ticket £37.00
      (Unlimited travel for 2 adults + 2 children)

Detailed Directions by Car:
The railway is situated just off the main A595 Western Lake District road.

RHIW VALLEY LIGHT RAILWAY

Address: Lower House Farm, Manafon, Nr. Welshpool   SY21 8BJ
Telephone Nº: None
Year Formed: 1971
Location of Line: By the side of the B4390 between Berriew and Manafon
Length of Line: ¾ mile

Nº of Steam Locos: 2
Nº of Other Locos: 1
Approx Nº of Visitors P.A.: 1,000
Gauge: 15 inches
Web site: www.rvlr.co.uk
E-mail: steam@rvlr.co.uk

GENERAL INFORMATION
Nearest Mainline Station: Welshpool (5 miles)
Nearest Bus Station: Welshpool (5 miles)
Car Parking: Available on site
Coach Parking: Available on site
Souvenir Shop(s): None
Food & Drinks: Available during operating days

SPECIAL INFORMATION
The Rhiw Valley Light Railway is planning projects to both extend the track and also construct a new waiting room.

OPERATING INFORMATION
Opening Times: 2015 operating dates:
23rd & 24th May; 6th & 7th June; 4th & 5th July; 1st & 2nd August; 5th & 6th September; 3rd & 4th October. Trains run from 12.00pm to 5.00pm.
Steam Working: During all operating days.
Prices: Adult £6.00
             Child £4.00 (Under-3s ride free)
             Concessions £5.00
             Family Tickets £20.00
                      (2 adults + 4 children)

Detailed Directions by Car:
Take the A483 south from Welshpool then, after 5 miles, turn right onto the B4390. Pass through Berriew and Pant-y-Ffridd and the railway is located at Lower House Farm on the outskirts of Manafon.

RHYL MINIATURE RAILWAY

Address: Marine Lake, Wellington Road, Rhyl LL18 1AQ	**Nº of Steam Locos**: 5
Telephone Nº: (01352) 759109	**Nº of Other Locos**: 3
E-mail: info@rhylminiaturerailway.co.uk	**Nº of Members**: Approximately 80
Year Formed: 1911	**Annual Membership Fee**: £8.00
Location of Line: Rhyl	**Approx Nº of Visitors P.A.**: 20,000
Length of Line: 1 mile	**Gauge**: 15 inches
	Web site: www.rhylminiaturerailway.co.uk

GENERAL INFORMATION

Nearest Mainline Station: Rhyl (1 mile)
Nearest Bus Station: Rhyl (1 mile)
Car Parking: Car Park near the Railway
Coach Parking: Available nearby
Souvenir Shop(s): Yes
Food & Drinks: Available

SPECIAL INFORMATION

The trust operates the oldest Miniature Railway in the UK. The principal locomotive and train have been operating there since the 1920's.

OPERATING INFORMATION

Opening Times: Every weekend from Easter until the end of September. Also on Bank Holiday Mondays, Fridays during June and July and daily during the School Summer Holidays. Trains run from 10.30am to 4.00pm.
Steam Working: Every Sunday and also Friday to Saturday during the School Summer Holidays.
Prices: Adult £2.50
          Child £1.50

Detailed Directions by Car:
From All Parts: The Railway is located behind the west end of Rhyl Promenade.

ROMNEY, HYTHE & DYMCHURCH RAILWAY

Address: New Romney Station, New Romney, Kent   TN28 8PL
Telephone Nº: (01797) 362353
Year Formed: 1927
Location of Line: Approximately 5 miles west of Folkestone
Length of Line: 13½ miles

Nº of Steam Locos: 11
Nº of Other Locos: 5
Nº of Members: 2,500
Annual Membership Fee: Supporters association – Adult £21.50
Approx Nº of Visitors P.A.: 160,000
Gauge: 15 inches
Web site: www.rhdr.org.uk

GENERAL INFORMATION

Nearest Mainline Station: Folkestone Central (5 miles) or Rye
Nearest Bus Station: Folkestone (then take the bus to Hythe)
Car Parking: Free parking at all major stations
Coach Parking: At New Romney & Dungeness
Souvenir Shop(s): Yes – 4 at various stations
Food & Drinks: 2 Cafes serving food and drinks plus a tea shop at Hythe Station.

SPECIAL INFORMATION

Opened in 1927 as 'The World's Smallest Public Railway'. Now the only 15" gauge tourist main line railway in the world. Double track, 7 stations.

OPERATING INFORMATION

Opening Times: 2015 dates: A daily service runs from 21st March to 1st November. Open at weekends in February, March and for Santa Specials during December. Also open daily during School half-terms.
Steam Working: All operational days.
Prices: Vary depending on length of journey.
Adult Day Rover £17.00
Child Day Rover £8.50 (Ages 3-15 years)
Concessionary Day Rover £15.00
Family Day Rover £45.00
(2 adults + 3 children)

Detailed Directions by Car:
Exit the M20 at Junction 11 then follow signs to Hythe and the brown tourist signs for the railway. Alternatively, Take the A259 to New Romney and follow the brown tourist signs for the railway.

ROYAL VICTORIA RAILWAY

Address: Royal Victoria Country Park, Netley, Southampton SO31 5GA	**Nº of Steam Locos:** 6
Telephone Nº: (023) 8045-6246	**Nº of Other Locos:** 5
Year Formed: 1995	**Approx Nº of Visitors P.A.:** Not known
Location of Line: Netley	**Gauge:** 10¼ inches
Length of Line: 1 mile	**Web site:** www.royalvictoriarailway.co.uk

GENERAL INFORMATION

Nearest Mainline Station: Netley
Nearest Bus Station: Southampton
Car Parking: Available on site – £3.00 fee
Coach Parking: Free parking available on site
Souvenir Shop(s): Yes
Food & Drinks: Yes

SPECIAL INFORMATION

The railway runs through the grounds of an old Victorian hospital and has good views of the Solent and the Isle of Wight. The Park covers 200 acres including woodland, grassland, beaches, picnic sites and a play area.

OPERATING INFORMATION

Opening Times: Weekends throughout the year and daily during local school holidays. Trains run from 11.00am to 4.30pm. The railway also opens by appointment for larger parties.
Steam Working: On special event days only. Please phone for further details.
Prices: Adult Return £1.75
Child Return £1.25
Note: Special rates are available for groups of 10 or more when pre-booked. Under-2s travel free.

Detailed Directions by Car:
From All Parts: Exit the M27 at Junction 8 and follow the Brown Tourist signs for the Royal Victoria Country Park. You will reach the Park after approximately 3 miles. Do not use Sat Nav as the directions will be incorrect!

RUDYARD LAKE STEAM RAILWAY

Address: Rudyard Station, Rudyard, Near Leek, Staffordshire ST13 8PF	**Nº of Steam Locos**: 6
Telephone Nº: (01538) 306704	**Nº of Other Locos**: 4
Year Formed: 1985	**Approx Nº of Visitors P.A.**: 50,000
Location: Rudyard to Hunthouse Wood	**Gauge**: 10¼ inches and 7¼ inches
Length of Line: 1½ miles	**Web site**: www.rlsr.org

GENERAL INFORMATION

Nearest Mainline Station: Stoke-on-Trent (10 miles)
Nearest Bus Station: Leek
Car Parking: Free parking at Rudyard Station
Coach Parking: Free parking at Rudyard Station
Souvenir Shop(s): Yes
Food & Drinks: Yes – Cafe open at weekends from April to October

SPECIAL INFORMATION

The Railway runs along the side of the historic Rudyard Lake that gave author Rudyard Kipling his name. "Drive a Steam Train" courses can be booked or bought as a gift with vouchers valid for 12 months. A short 7¼ inch gauge railway also operates on special event days.

OPERATING INFORMATION

Opening Times: 2015 dates: Every Sunday and Bank Holiday from March to the end of November. Also open on every Saturday from 21st March to 7th November and daily from 1st to 12th April, 25th to 29th May, 22nd July to 6th September and 26th to 30th October. Also open on Wednesdays in June, July and September and there is a Steam Gala on 19th and 20th September.
Steam Working: All trains are normally steam hauled. Trains run from 11.00am and the last train runs at 4.00pm.
Prices: Adult Return £4.00
Child Return £2.50
Other fares and Day Rover tickets are also available.

Detailed Directions by Car:
From All Parts: Head for Leek then follow the A523 North towards Macclesfield for 1 mile. Follow the brown tourist signs to the B5331 signposted for Rudyard for ½ mile. Pass under the Railway bridge and turn immediately left and go up the ramp to the Station car park.

RUISLIP LIDO RAILWAY

Address: Reservoir Road, Ruislip,
Middlesex HA4 7TY
Telephone Nº: (01895) 622595
Year Formed: 1979
Location of Line: Trains travel from
Ruislip Lido to Woody Bay
Length of Line: 1¼ miles

Nº of Steam Locos: 1
Nº of Other Locos: 5
Nº of Members: 166
Annual Membership Fee: £15.00 (Adult)
Approx Nº of Visitors P.A.: 60,000
Gauge: 12 inches
Web site: www.ruisliplidorailway.org

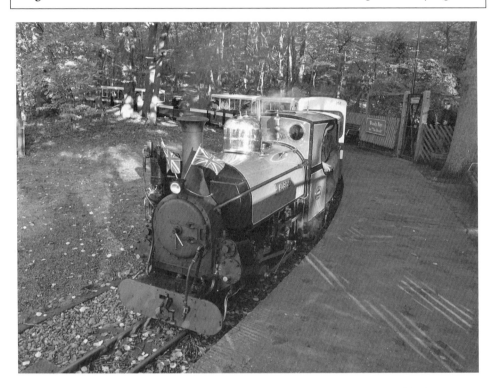

GENERAL INFORMATION

Nearest Mainline Station: West Ruislip (2 miles)
Nearest Bus Station: Ruislip Underground Station
Car Parking: Free parking available at the Lido
Coach Parking: Free parking available at the Lido
Souvenir Shop(s): Yes
Food & Drinks: A Cafe is open on weekends and
Bank Holidays. A Pub/Restaurant is open daily.

SPECIAL INFORMATION

The steam locomotive, 'Mad Bess' used by Ruislip
Lido Railway was actually built by the members over
a 12 year period!

OPERATING INFORMATION

Opening Times: 2015 dates: Weekends from 14th
February to 29th November. Daily from 28th March
to 12th April then 22nd July to 1st September. Please
contact the railway for details about services
running during December and January.
Steam Working: See above.
Prices: Adult Return £3.00 (Single fare £2.00)
Child Return £2.50 (Single fare £1.50)
Family Return £9.00 (Single fare £6.00)
(2 adults + 2 children)
Note: Under-3s travel for free

Detailed Directions by Car:
From All Parts: Follow the signs from the A40 and take the A4180 through Ruislip before turning left onto the
B469.

SALTBURN MINIATURE RAILWAY

Address: Valley Gardens, Saltburn	**Nº of Steam Locos**: Visiting locos only
Telephone Nº: 07813 153975	**Nº of Other Locos**: 3
Year Formed: 1947	**Nº of Members**: 12
Location of Line: Cat Nab to Forest Halt	**Annual Membership Fee**: £1.00
Stations, Saltburn	**Approx Nº of Visitors P.A.**: 20,000
Length of Line: ¾ mile	**Gauge**: 15 inches
Web site: www.saltburn-miniature-railway.org.uk	

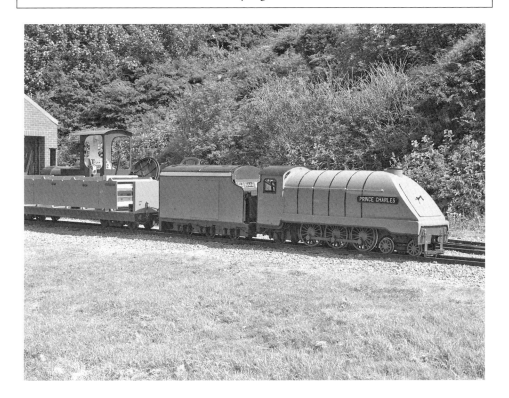

GENERAL INFORMATION

Nearest Mainline Station: Saltburn (½ mile)
Nearest Bus Station: Saltburn (½ mile)
Car Parking: Available at Cat Nab Station
Coach Parking: Glen Side (at the top of the bank)
Souvenir Shop(s): At Cat Nab Station
Food & Drinks: None

E-mail: saltburn.miniaturerailway@ntlworld.com

OPERATING INFORMATION

Opening Times: Weekends and Bank Holidays from Easter until the end of September. Also open Tuesday to Friday during the Summer School Holidays. All services operate weather permitting. Trains run from 1.00pm to 5.00pm.
Steam Working: Please contact the railway for details.
Prices: Adult Return £2.00 (Adult Single £1.00)
Child Return 1.00 (Child Single 50p)
Note: Family tickets and frequent user discounts are also available. Under-5s ride free of charge.

Detailed Directions by Car:
Follow the A174 from Middlesbrough (West) or Whitby (East) to Saltburn-by-the-Sea. Cat Nab Station with its adjoining car park is situated by the beach, directly off the C74 (C174).

SHERWOOD FOREST RAILWAY

Address: Gorsethorpe Lane, Edwinstowe, Mansfield NG21 9HL	**Nº of Steam Locos:** 2
Telephone Nº: (01623) 515339	**Nº of Other Locos:** 3
Year Formed: 1999	**Nº of Members:** 13
Location of Line: Between Mansfield Woodhouse and Edwinstowe	**Approx Nº of Visitors P.A.:** 5,000
	Gauge: 15 inches
Length of Line: 680 yards	**Website:** www.sherwoodforestrailway.com

GENERAL INFORMATION

Nearest Mainline Station: Mansfield (7 miles)
Nearest Bus Station: Mansfield (7 miles)
Car Parking: Free parking available on site
Coach Parking: Available on site
Souvenir Shop(s): Yes
Food & Drinks: Available

SPECIAL INFORMATION

The Railway runs through the grounds of Shaw-Browne Estates which has play areas for children and picnic areas. Check out the web site for up-to-date news.

OPERATING INFORMATION

Opening Times: 2015 dates: Open daily from 7th March through to the end of October. Trains run from 11.00am to 4.30pm on most days.
Steam Working: Every operating day.
Prices: Adults £2.00
Chidren £2.00

Detailed Directions by Car:
From the A1: Turn off at the Worksop roundabout and head to Ollerton. Follow the A6075 through Edwinstowe and towards Mansfield Woodhouse, then turn left at the double mini-roundabout. The Farm Park is on the right after approximately 200 yards; From Nottingham: Head to Ollerton, then as above; From the M1: Exit at Junction 27 and head into Mansfield. Follow signs to Mansfield Woodhouse and then on towards Edwinstowe. From here, follow the tourist signs for the Steam Railway.

SITTINGBOURNE & KEMSLEY LIGHT RAILWAY

Address: P.O. Box 300, Sittingbourne, Kent   ME10 2DZ
Info/Talking Timetable: (01795) 424899
Year Formed: 1969
Location of Line: North of Sittingbourne
Length of Line: 2 miles

Nº of Steam Locos: 9 (2 Standard gauge)
Nº of Other Locos: 3
Nº of Members: 300
Annual Membership Fee: £18.00
Approx Nº of Visitors P.A.: 6,000
Gauge: 2 feet 6 inches
Web site: www.sklr.net

GENERAL INFORMATION

Nearest Mainline Station: Sittingbourne (¼ mile)
Nearest Bus Station: Sittingbourne Mainline station
Car Parking: Sittingbourne Retail Park (behind KFC)
Coach Parking: Sittingbourne Retail Park
Souvenir Shop(s): Yes
Food & Drinks: Yes

SPECIAL INFORMATION

The railway is the only original preserved narrow gauge industrial steam railway in S.E. England (formerly the Bowaters Paper Company Railway). The railway celebrated 100 years of Steam locomotion in 2005 and the line includes a trip along a ½ mile concrete viaduct. Other attractions include a Museum, Model Railways, a Children's play area and a Wildlife Garden.

OPERATING INFORMATION

Opening Times: Sundays and Bank Holiday weekends from April to September. Also open on Wednesdays in August and for Santa Specials on weekends in December. Phone for details of Special Events held throughout the year.
Steam Working: Trains run from 1.00pm normally, but from 11.00am on Bank Holiday weekends and Sundays in August. Last train runs at 4.00pm (except for during some special events).
Prices: Adult Return £6.00
　　　　　　Child Return £3.00
　　　　　　Senior Citizen Return £4.00
　　　　　　Family Return £17.00
Note: Different fares may apply on special event days.

Detailed Directions by Car:
From East or West: Take the M2 (or M20) to A249 and travel towards Sittingbourne. Take the A2 to Sittingbourne town and continue to the roundabout outside the Mainline station. Take the turning onto the B2006 (Milton Regis) under the Mainline bridge and the car park entrance for the Railway is by the next roundabout, behind McDonalds, in the Sittingbourne Retail Park.

SNOWDON MOUNTAIN RAILWAY

Address: Llanberis, Caernarfon, Gwynedd, Wales LL55 4TY	**Length of Line**: 4¾ miles
Telephone Nº: 0844 493-8120	**Nº of Steam Locos**: 4
Fax Nº: (01286) 872518	**Nº of Other Locos**: 4
Year Formed: 1894	**Approx Nº of Visitors P.A.**: 140,000
Location of Line: Llanberis to the summit of Snowdon	**Gauge**: 2 feet 7½ inches
	Web site: www.snowdonrailway.co.uk

GENERAL INFORMATION

Nearest Mainline Station: Bangor (9 miles)
Nearest Bus Station: Caernarfon (7½ miles)
Car Parking: Llanberis Station car park – pay and display. Also other car parks nearby.
Coach Parking: As above but space is very limited
Souvenir Shop(s): Yes
Food & Drinks: Yes

SPECIAL INFORMATION

Britain's only public rack and pinion railway climbs to within 60 feet of the 3,560 feet peak of Snowdon, the highest mountain in England and Wales. The Diesel and Steam Experiences are both 2½ hour return journeys to the summit.

OPERATING INFORMATION

Opening Times: 2015 dates: Open daily (weather permitting) from 20th March until 1st November. Trains depart at regular intervals from 9.00am. The last departure can be as late as 5.00pm depending on demand. It is advisable to guarantee tickets and book in advance either on-line or by telephone.
Steam Working: Ride the "Snowdon Lily" or the new "Mountain Goat" as part of the Heritage Steam Experience operating from May to September. Please contact the railway for further details.
Prices: Adult Summit Return £27.00 (Diesel)
　　　　　　　Adult Summit Return £35.00 (Steam)
　　　　　　　Child Summit Return £18.00 (Diesel)
　　　　　　　Child Summit Return £25.00 (Steam)

Detailed Directions by Car:
Llanberis Station is situated on the A4086 Caernarfon to Capel Curig road, 7½ miles from Caernarfon. Convenient access via the main North Wales coast road (A55). Exit at the A55/A5 junction and follow signs to Llanberis via B4366, B4547 and A4086.

SOUTH DOWNS LIGHT RAILWAY

Address: South Downs Light Railway, Stopham Road, Pulborough RH20 1DS	**Nº of Steam Locos**: 8
Telephone Nº: 07518 753784	**Nº of Other Locos**: 2
Year Formed: 1999	**Nº of Members**: 60
Location: Pulborough Garden Centre	**Annual Membership Fee**: Adult £20.00
Length of Line: 1 kilometre	**Approx Nº of Visitors P.A.**: 18,000
	Gauge: 10¼ inches
	Web site: www.south-downs-railway.com

GENERAL INFORMATION

Nearest Mainline Station: Pulborough (½ mile)
Nearest Bus Station: Bus stop just outside Centre
Car Parking: Free parking on site
Coach Parking: Free parking on site
Souvenir Shop(s): Yes
Food & Drinks: Yes – in the Garden Restaurant

SPECIAL INFORMATION

The members of the Society own and operate a large collection of 10¼ inch gauge locomotives.
The Railway is located within the Pulborough Garden Centre.

OPERATING INFORMATION

Opening Times: Weekends and Bank Holidays from March until September, Wednesdays in School Holidays and also Santa Specials at weekends in December. Trains run from 11.00am to 3.30pm.
Steam Working: Most services are steam hauled.
Prices: Adult £1.50
Child £1.00 (Under-2s travel free of charge)
Note: Supersaver tickets are also available and a special 'South Downs Belle' runs on the first Sunday of each month.

Detailed Directions by Car:
From All Parts: The Centre is situated on the A283, ½ mile west of Pulborough. Pulborough itself is on the A29 London to Bognor Regis Road.

SOUTHEND PIER RAILWAY

Address: Western Esplanade, Southend-on-Sea SS1 1EE
Telephone Nº: (01702) 618747
Year Formed: 1889
Location of Line: Southend seafront
Length of Line: 2,180 yards

Nº of Steam Locos: None
Nº of Other Locos: 2
Approx Nº of Visitors P.A.: 300,000
Gauge: 3 feet
Web site: http://www.southend.gov.uk/ info/200306/southend_pier

GENERAL INFORMATION

Nearest Mainline Station: Southend Central (¼ mile)
Nearest Bus Station: Southend (¼ mile)
Car Parking: Available on the seafront
Coach Parking: Available
Souvenir Shop(s): Yes
Food & Drinks: Available

SPECIAL INFORMATION

The railway takes passengers to the end of Southend Pier which, at 1.33 miles, is the longest pleasure pier in the world.

OPERATING INFORMATION

Opening Times: Daily except for Christmas Day. Times vary depending on the season – trains run from 8.30am to 7.00pm during the Summer.
Steam Working: None.
Prices: Adult Return £4.00
Child Return £2.00
Concessionary Return £2.00
Family Return Ticket £10.00

Detailed Directions by Car:
From All Parts: Take the A127 to Southend and follow the brown tourist signs to the Pier.

SOUTH TYNEDALE RAILWAY

Address: The Railway Station, Alston, Cumbria CA9 3JB	**Nº of Steam Locos:** 4
Telephone Nº: (01434) 382828	**Nº of Other Locos:** 4
Year Formed: 1973	**Nº of Members:** 362
Location of Line: From Alston, northwards along South Tyne Valley to Lintley	**Annual Membership Fee:** £22.00 (Adult)
	Approx Nº of Visitors P.A.: 22,000
Length of Line: 3½ miles	**Gauge:** 2 feet
	Web: www.south-tynedale-railway.org.uk

GENERAL INFORMATION

Nearest Mainline Station: Haltwhistle (15 miles)
Nearest Bus Stop: Alston Townfoot (¼ mile)
Car Parking: Free parking at Alston Station but limited spaces available at Lintley Station
Coach Parking: Free parking at Alston Station but a coach drop off point only at Lintley Station
Souvenir Shop(s): Yes
Food & Drinks: The Buffer Stop Cafe is open on operating days and a buffet car runs on some services

SPECIAL INFORMATION

The railway operates along part of the old Alston to Haltwhistle branch line in the South Tyne Valley. A further extension to Slaggyford is planned by 2017.

OPERATING INFORMATION

Opening Times: 2015 dates: Bank Holidays, weekends and daily during School Holidays from 3rd April until the 31st October. Please check the railway's website for information about other running dates including Special Events including the Santa Express which operates during December.
Steam Working: Please contact the railway for information about steam working.
Prices: Adult Return £10.00; Adult Single £5.00
Child Return £4.00; Child Single £2.00
Family Return Ticket £24.00
(2 Adults + 3 Children)
Children under 3 travel free
Dogs £2.00

Detailed Directions by Car:
Alston can be reached by a number of roads from various directions including A689, A686 and the B6277. Alston Station is situated just off the A686 Hexham road, north of Alston Town Centre. Look for the brown tourist signs on roads into Alston. Lintley Station is signposted off the A689.

STEEPLE GRANGE LIGHT RAILWAY

Address: High Peak Trail, Near National Stone Centre, Wirksworth DE4 4LS
Telephone Nº: (01629) 55123 (Evenings)
Year Formed: 1986
Location of Line: Off the High Peak trail near Wirksworth
Length of Line: ½ mile at present

Nº of Steam Locos: None at present
Nº of Other Locos: 16
Nº of Members: 200
Annual Membership Fee: From £8.00
Approx Nº of Visitors P.A.: 8,000+
Gauge: 18 inches
Web site: www.steeplegrange.co.uk

GENERAL INFORMATION

Nearest Mainline Station: Cromford (2 miles)
Nearest Bus Station: Matlock
Car Parking: Available nearby
Coach Parking: Available nearby
Souvenir Shop(s): Yes
Food & Drinks: Light refreshments available

SPECIAL INFORMATION

The Railway is built on the track bed of the former Standard Gauge Cromford and High Peak Railway branch to Middleton. The railway uses mostly former mining/quarrying rolling stock and has two separate lines operating.

OPERATING INFORMATION

Opening Times: Sundays and Bank Holidays from Easter until the end of October. Also open on Saturdays in July and August and on other days by prior arrangement. Special Events at other times of the year including Santa Specials during December. Please contact the railway for further information. Trains run from 12.00pm to 5.00pm
Steam Working: None at present
Prices: Adult Return £4.00   Child Return £2.00
Senior Citizen Return £3.00
Family Return £10.00
Note: Special fares apply during special events and also for group bookings.

Detailed Directions by Car:
The Railway is situated adjacent to the National Stone Centre just to the north of Wirksworth at the junction of the B5035 and B5036. Car parking is available at the National Stone Centre and in Old Porter Lane.

SUTTON HALL RAILWAY

Address: Tabors Farm, Sutton Hall, Shopland Road, near Rochford, Essex SS4 1LQ	**Nº of Steam Locos:** 1
	Nº of Other Locos: 1
	Nº of Members: Approximately 8
Telephone Nº: (01702) 334337	**Annual Membership Fee:** £15.00
Year Formed: 1997	**Approx Nº of Visitors P.A.:** 3,500
Location of Line: Sutton Hall Farm	**Gauge:** 10¼ inches
Length of Line: Almost 1 mile	**Web site:** None at present

GENERAL INFORMATION

Nearest Mainline Station: Rochford (1½ miles)
Nearest Bus Station: Rochford
Car Parking: Free parking available on site
Coach Parking: Free parking available on site
Souvenir Shop(s): None
Food & Drinks: Drinks and snacks available

SPECIAL INFORMATION

The Railway was bought by C. Tabor in 1985 for use with his Farm Barn Dances. The Sutton Hall Railway Society was formed in 1997 (with C. Tabor as Society President) and now opens the line for public running on some Sundays. The railway is staffed entirely by Volunteer Members of the Society.

OPERATING INFORMATION

Opening Times: Open the 4th Sunday in the month from April until September, 12.00pm to 6.00pm. Specials run on Easter Sunday afternoon, Halloween evening (5.00pm to 10.00pm) and a Santa Special on the afternoon of the first Sunday in December (12.00pm to 5.00pm).
Steam Working: All operating days.
Prices: Adult Return £2.00
Child Return £1.50

Detailed Directions by Car:
From Southend Airport (A127 Southend to London Main Route & A1159): At the Airport Roundabout (with the McDonalds on the left) go over the railway bridge signposted for Rochford. At the 1st roundabout turn right (Ann Boleyn Pub on the right) into Sutton Road. Continue straight on at the mini-roundabout then when the road forks turn left into Shopland Road signposted for Barling and Great Wakering. Turn right after approximately 400 yards into the long tree-lined road for Sutton Hall Farm.

TALYLLYN RAILWAY

Address: Wharf Station, Tywyn, Gwynedd, LL36 9EY	**N° of Steam Locos:** 6
Telephone N°: (01654) 710472	**N° of Other Locos:** 4
E-mail: enquiries@talyllyn.co.uk	**N° of Members:** 3,500
Year Formed: 1865	**Annual Membership Fee:** Adult £25.00
Location of Line: Tywyn to Nant Gwernol	**Approx N° of Visitors P.A.:** 50,000
Length of Line: 7¼ miles	**Gauge:** 2 feet 3 inches
	Web site: www.talyllyn.co.uk

GENERAL INFORMATION

Nearest Mainline Station: Tywyn (300 yards)
Nearest Bus Station: Tywyn (300 yards)
Car Parking: 100 yards away
Coach Parking: Free parking (100 yards)
Souvenir Shop(s): Yes
Food & Drinks: Yes

SPECIAL INFORMATION

Talyllyn Railway was the first preserved railway in the world – saved from closure in 1951. The railway was originally opened in 1866 to carry slate from Bryn Eglwys Quarry to Tywyn. Among the railway's attractions are a Narrow Gauge Railway Museum at the Tywyn Wharf terminus.

OPERATING INFORMATION

Opening Times: 2015 dates: Daily from 28th March to 1st November. Also open on other selected dates in February, March, November and December including most weekends. Generally open from 10.30am to 5.00pm. Please contact the railway or check the web site for further details.
Steam Working: All services are steam-hauled.
Prices: Adult Return £18.00 (Day Rover ticket)
Senior Citizen Return £16.00
Children (ages 5-15) pay £2.00 if travelling with an adult. Otherwise, they pay half adult fare. Children under the age of 5 travel free of charge.
Note: The prices shown include a voluntary donation under the Gift Aid scheme. Standard tickets are also available at slightly lower prices.

Detailed Directions by Car:
From the North: Take the A493 from Dolgellau into Tywyn; From the South: Take the A493 from Machynlleth to Tywyn.

Teifi Valley Railway

Address: Henllan Station, Henllan, near Newcastle Emlyn SA44 5TD	**N° of Steam Locos**: 2
Telephone N°: (01559) 371077	**N° of Other Locos**: 3
Year Formed: 1978	**N° of Members**: Approximately 150
Location of Line: Between Cardigan and Carmarthen off the A484	**Annual Membership Fee**: £18.00
	Approx N° of Visitors P.A.: 15,000
Length of Line: 2 miles	**Gauge**: 2 feet
	Web site: www.teifivalleyrailway.org

GENERAL INFORMATION

Nearest Mainline Station: Carmarthen (10 miles)
Nearest Bus Station: Carmarthen (10 miles)
Car Parking: Spaces for 70 cars available.
Coach Parking: Spaces for 4 coaches available.
Souvenir Shop(s): Yes
Food & Drinks: Yes – Cafe is open on weekends

SPECIAL INFORMATION

The Railway was formerly part of the G.W.R. but now runs on a Narrow Gauge using Quarry Engines.

OPERATING INFORMATION

Opening Times: 2015 dates: Open from Sunday to Thursday and on Bank Holidays in April, May, June July, August and September. Trains run from 11.15am to 3.00pm (or 4.45pm in August).
Steam Working: Most operating days – please phone the Railway for further details.
Prices: Adult £7.50
             Child £5.00
Note: The railway experienced severe operating issues during 2014 but these are expected to be resolved by the start of 2015 season.

Detailed Directions by Car:
From All Parts: The Railway is situated in the Village of Henllan between the A484 and the A475 (on the B4334) about 4 miles east of Newcastle Emlyn.

THRELKELD QUARRY RAILWAY

Address: Threlkeld Quarry & Mining Museum, Threlkeld, Near Keswick, CA12 4TT
Telephone N°: (01768) 779747
Year Formed: 2010
Location of Line: Cumbria
Length of Line: ½ mile

N° of Steam Locos: 1
N° of Other Locos: 8
Approx N° of Visitors P.A.: 20,000
Gauge: 2 feet
Web: www.threlkeldminingmuseum.co.uk

GENERAL INFORMATION

Nearest Mainline Station: Penrith (14 miles)
Nearest Bus Station: Keswick (5 miles)
Car Parking: Available on site
Coach Parking: Available
Souvenir Shop(s): Yes
Food & Drinks: Available

SPECIAL INFORMATION

Underground tours are available for an extra charge. Demonstration Working Weekends in conjunction with the Vintage Excavator Trust are held on the third weekend in May and September.

OPERATING INFORMATION

Opening Times: Daily from Easter to the end of October half-term. Santa Specials also run on dates in December. Please contact the Museum for details. Open from 10.00am to 5.00pm.
Steam Working: During the School Holidays and on Bank Holiday weekends. A Steam Gala is held on the last weekend in July.
Prices: Adult Museum Entry £3.00   Rides £3.00
　　　　　Child Museum Entry £1.50   Rides £1.50

Detailed Directions by Car:
From All Parts: Exit the M6 at Junction 40 and take the A66 towards Keswick. Turn off onto the B5322 at Threlkeld and follow signs for the Mining Museum.

TODDINGTON NARROW GAUGE RAILWAY

Address: The Station, Toddington, Cheltenham, Gloucestershire   GL54 5DT
Telephone Nº: (01242) 621405
Year Formed: 1985
Location of Line: 5 miles south of Broadway, Worcestershire, near the A46
Length of Line: ½ mile

Nº of Steam Locos: 4
Nº of Other Locos: 5
Nº of Members: Approximately 50
Annual Membership Fee: £6.00
Approx Nº of Visitors P.A.: 2,000
Gauge: 2 feet
Web site: www.gwsr.com (recommended) or www.toddington-narrow-gauge.co.uk

GENERAL INFORMATION

Nearest Mainline Station: Cheltenham Spa or Ashchurch
Nearest Bus Station: Cheltenham
Car Parking: Parking available at Toddington, Winchcombe & Cheltenham Racecourse Stations
Coach Parking: Parking available as above
Souvenir Shop(s): None
Food & Drinks: None at the TNGR itself but available at the adjacent GWSR site.

SPECIAL INFORMATION

The railway currently has two German-built World War One Henschel locomotive trench engines.

OPERATING INFORMATION

Opening Times: 2015 dates: Sundays and Bank Holidays from April to September inclusive. Also some Saturdays during these months and on Wednesdays during August. A number of Special Event weekends operate throughout the season. Please contact the railway for details. Trains usually run from every 35 minutes from around noon.
Steam Working: Please check the GWSR web site for further information.
Prices: Adults £3.00
Children £1.00 (Under-5s ride free)

Detailed Directions by Car:
Toddington is 11 miles north east of Cheltenham, 5 miles south of Broadway just off the B4632 (old A46). Exit the M5 at Junction 9 towards Stow-on-the-Wold for the B4632. The Railway is clearly visible from the B4632.

VALE OF RHEIDOL RAILWAY

Address: Park Avenue, Aberystwyth, Ceredigion SY23 1PG
Telephone Nº: (01970) 625819
Year Formed: 1902
Location of Line: Aberystwyth to Devil's Bridge
Length of Line: 11¾ miles

Nº of Steam Locos: 3
Nº of Other Locos: 1
Approx Nº of Visitors P.A.: 50,000
Gauge: 1 foot 11¾ inches
Web site: www.rheidolrailway.co.uk

GENERAL INFORMATION

Nearest Mainline Station: Aberystwyth (adjacent)
Nearest Bus Station: Aberystwyth (adjacent)
Car Parking: Available on site
Coach Parking: Parking available on site
Souvenir Shops: At Devil's Bridge and Aberystwyth
Food & Drinks: At Devil's Bridge and Aberystwyth

SPECIAL INFORMATION

The journey between the stations take one hour in each direction. At Devil's Bridge there is a cafe, toilets, a picnic area and the famous Mynach Falls. The line climbs over 600 feet in 11¾ miles. Look out for the Red Kites and Buzzards flying overhead!

OPERATING INFORMATION

Opening Times: 2015 dates: Regular services run daily from 28th March to 1st November (but closed on most Fridays in October). Trains also run on Sundays in November and Santa Specials operate on dates during December. Please check the web site or phone the railway for further information.
Steam Working: All trains are steam-hauled.
Prices: Adult Return £18.00
Senior Citizen Return £17.00
Accompanied Child Return £6.00
Unaccompanied Child Return £9.00
Note: Trains can be chartered by arrangement at other times of the year.

Detailed Directions by Car:
From the North take A487 into Aberystwyth. From the East take A470 and A44 to Aberystwyth. From the South take A487 or A485 to Aberystwyth. The Station is located in the centre of town near the 'Park and Ride' site.

Volks Electric Railway

Address: Arch 285, Madeira Drive, Brighton BN2 1EN	**N° of Steam Locos**: None
Telephone N°: (01273) 292718	**N° of Other Locos**: 7
Year Formed: 1883	**Approx N° of Visitors P.A.**: 250,000
Location of Line: Brighton seafront	**Gauge**: 2 feet 8½ inches
Length of Line: 1 mile	**Web site**: www.volkselectricrailway.co.uk

GENERAL INFORMATION

Nearest Mainline Station: Brighton (2 miles)
Nearest Bus Station: Brighton Pier (¼ mile)
Car Parking: Available on site
Coach Parking: Available
Souvenir Shop(s): Yes
Food & Drinks: Available

SPECIAL INFORMATION

Opened in 1883, Volk's Electric Railway is the world's oldest operating electric railway. The brainchild of inventor Magnus Volk, the railway runs for just over a mile along Brighton seafront between Aquarium (for Brighton Pier) and Black Rock (for the Marina).

OPERATING INFORMATION

Opening Times: 2015 dates: Open daily from 28th March to 30th September, usually from 10.15am to 5.00pm (11.15am starts on Tuesdays and Fridays). Services run until 6.00pm on weekends and Bank Holidays.
Steam Working: None
Prices: Adult Return £3.70 (Single £2.80)
Child Return £2.20 (Single £1.70)
Concessionary Return £2.80 (Single £2.10)
Family Return £9.50 (Single £7.10)

Detailed Directions by Car:
From All Parts: Take the A23/A27 to Brighton. The railway is located on the seafront next to the Pier and Wheel.

WATFORD MINIATURE RAILWAY

Address: Cassiobury Park, Watford, WD17 7LB	**Nº of Steam Locos:** None
Telephone Nº: 07511 749248	**Nº of Other Locos:** 2
Year Formed: 1959	**Approx Nº of Visitors P.A.:** 25,000
Location: At the northern end of Cassiobury Park, Watford	**Gauge:** 10¼ inches
Length of Line: 600 yards	**Web site:** None

GENERAL INFORMATION

Nearest Mainline Station: Watford Junction (appoximately 1½ miles)
Nearest Tube Station: Watford (400 yards)
Car Parking: Limited spaces available at the Park.
Coach Parking: None
Souvenir Shop(s): None
Food & Drinks: Cafe available in the Park.

OPERATING INFORMATION

Opening Times: Weekends and School Holidays between 11.30pm and 5.00pm.
Steam Working: None
Prices: All fares: £1.50 per ride

Detailed Directions by Car:
Exit the M25 at Junction 19 or 20 and follow the A41 to Watford. Turn right at the Dome Roundabout heading southwards on the A412 St. Albans Road and continue through Watford Town Centre onto the A412 Rickmansworth Road. Turn right onto Cassiobury Park Avenue, following the brown information sign and continue to the end of the road for the car park.

WAVENEY VALLEY RAILWAY

Address: Bressingham Steam Museum, Bressingham, Diss, Norfolk IP22 2AB **Telephone Nº**: (01379) 686900 **Year Formed**: Mid 1950's **Location of Line**: Bressingham, Near Diss **Length of Line**: 5 miles in total (3 lines)	**Nº of Steam Locos**: Many Steam locos **Nº of Members**: 70 volunteers **Approx Nº of Visitors P.A.**: 80,000+ **Gauge**: Standard, 2 foot, 10¼ inches and 15 inches **Web site**: www.bressingham.co.uk

GENERAL INFORMATION

Nearest Mainline Station: Diss (2½ miles)
Nearest Bus Station: Bressingham (1¼ miles)
Car Parking: Free parking for 400 cars available
Coach Parking: Free parking for 30 coaches
Souvenir Shop(s): Yes
Food & Drinks: Yes

SPECIAL INFORMATION

The railway operates at the Bressingham Steam Museum which, in addition to Steam locomotives, has a large selection of steam traction engines, fixed steam engines, the National Dad's Army Museum, two extensive gardens and a water garden centre.

OPERATING INFORMATION

Opening Times: 2015 dates: Daily from 26th March to 1st November. Open from 10.30am to 5.00pm and until 5.30pm in June, July and August.
Steam Working: Almost every operating day except for most Mondays and Tuesdays in March, April, May, June, July, September and October. Please phone the Museum for further details.
Prices: Adult £11.49 (non-Steam) £13.99 (Steam)
Child £7.49 (non-Steam) £9.99 (Steam)
Seniors £10.49 (non-Steam) £12.59 (Steam)
Note: Reduced entry charges are available for visitors who do not take railway rides. The prices shown include an optional donation of 10%.

Detailed Directions by Car:
From All Parts: Take the A11 to Thetford and then follow the A1066 towards Diss for Bressingham. The Museum is signposted by the brown tourist signs.

WELLS HARBOUR RAILWAY

Address: Wells Harbour Railway,
Pinewoods, Beach Road,
Wells-next-the-Sea   NR23 1DR
Telephone Nº: (07939) 149264
Year Formed: 1976
Location of Line: Wells-next-the-Sea
Length of Line: Approximately 1 mile

Nº of Steam Locos: None
Nº of Other Locos: 3
Approx Nº of Visitors P.A.: 50,000
Gauge: 10¼ inches
Web site: None

GENERAL INFORMATION

Nearest Mainline Station: King's Lynn (21 miles)
Nearest Bus Station: Norwich (24 miles)
Car Parking: Public car parks near each station
Coach Parking: Available in town
Souvenir Shop(s): No
Food & Drinks: No

SPECIAL INFORMATION

Wells Harbour Railway was the first 10¼" narrow
gauge railway to run a scheduled passenger service
and is listed in the Guinness Book of Records!

OPERATING INFORMATION

Opening Times: Weekends from Easter until Spring
Bank Holiday then daily through to the middle of
September. Then weekends until the end of October.
The first train departs at 10.30am.
Steam Working: None
Prices: Adult Single £1.70
          Child Single £1.00

Detailed Directions by Car:

Wells-next-the-Sea is located on the North Norfolk cost between Hunstanton and Cromer. The railway is situated
on Beach Road next to the harbour. Follow the signs for Pinewoods and Beach.

WELLS & WALSINGHAM LIGHT RAILWAY

Address: The Station, Wells-next-the-Sea NR23 1QB	**Nº of Steam Locos**: 2
Telephone Nº: (01328) 711630	**Nº of Other Locos**: 2
Year Formed: 1982	**Nº of Members**: 50
Location of Line: Wells-next-the-Sea to Walsingham, Norfolk	**Annual Membership Fee**: £11.00
Length of Line: 4 miles	**Approx Nº of Visitors P.A.**: 20,000
	Gauge: 10¼ inches
	Website: www.wellswalsinghamrailway.co.uk

GENERAL INFORMATION

Nearest Mainline Station: King's Lynn (21 miles)
Nearest Bus Station: Norwich (24 miles)
Car Parking: Free parking at site
Coach Parking: Free parking at site
Souvenir Shop(s): Yes
Food & Drinks: Yes

SPECIAL INFORMATION

The Railway is the longest 10¼ inch narrow-gauge steam railway in the world. The course of the railway is famous for wildlife and butterflies in season.

OPERATING INFORMATION

Opening Times: 2015 dates: Daily from 28th March until 1st November.
Steam Working: Trains run from either 10.30am or on most operating days (10.15am during August).
Prices: Adult Return £9.00
Child Return £7.00 (Under-4s ride free)

Detailed Directions by Car:
Wells-next-the-Sea is situated on the North Norfolk Coast midway between Hunstanton and Cromer. The Main Station is situated on the main A149 Stiffkey Road. Follow the brown tourist signs for the Railway.

WELSH HIGHLAND HERITAGE RAILWAY

Address: Tremadog Road, Porthmadog, Gwynedd LL49 9DY
Telephone Nº: (01766) 513402
Year Formed: 1961
Location of Line: Opposite Porthmadog Mainline Station
Length of Line: 1½ mile round trip

Nº of Steam Locos: 3
Nº of Other Locos: 18
Nº of Members: 1,000
Annual Membership Fee: £30.00 Adult
Approx Nº of Visitors P.A.: 25,000
Gauge: 1 foot 11½ inches
Web site: www.whr.co.uk

GENERAL INFORMATION

Nearest Mainline Station: Porthmadog (adjacent)
Nearest Bus Station: Services 1 & 3 stop 50 yards away
Car Parking: Free parking at site, plus a public Pay and Display car park within 100 yards
Coach Parking: Adjacent
Souvenir Shop(s): Yes – large range available
Food & Drinks: Yes – excellent home cooking at the Russell Team Room!

SPECIAL INFORMATION

The Welsh Highland Railway is a family-orientated attraction based around a Railway Heritage Centre and includes a guided, hands-on tour of the sheds.

OPERATING INFORMATION

Opening Times: 2015 dates: Daily from 28th April to 31st October except for some Mondays and Fridays during October. Trains run at 10.30am, 11.30am, 1.00pm, 2.00pm, 3.00pm and 4.00pm (the last train runs at 3.00pm during October and November).
Steam Working: Most days during the School Holidays and on other selected weekends. Please check with the railway for further details.
Prices: Adult Day Rover £8.50
Child Day Rover £4.25   (Under-5s free)
Senior Citizen Day Rover £7.50
Family Day Rover £19.50
(2 adults + 2 children)

Detailed Directions by Car:
From Bangor/Caernarfon take the A487 to Porthmadog. From Pwllheli take the A497 to Porthmadog then turn left at the roundabout. From the Midlands take A487 to Portmadog. Once in Porthmadog, follow the brown tourist signs. The line is located right next to Porthmadog Mainline Station, opposite the Queens Hotel.

WELSH HIGHLAND RAILWAY

Postal Address: Ffestiniog Railway, Harbour Station, Porthmadog LL49 9NF	**Nº of Steam Locos**: 8 (5 working)
Telephone Nº: (01766) 516000	**Nº of Other Locos**: 3
Year Formed: 1997	**Nº of Members**: 2,300
Location: Caernarfon to Porthmadog	**Annual Membership Fee**: £23.00
Length of Line: 25 miles	**Approx Nº of Visitors P.A.**: 360,000
Web site: www.festrail.co.uk	**Gauge**: 1 foot 11½ inches
	E-mail: enquiries@festrail.co.uk

GENERAL INFO

Nearest Mainline Station:
Porthmadog (½ mile) or Bangor (7 miles) (Bus service Nº 5 to Caernarfon)
Nearest Bus Station:
Porthmadog or Caernarfon
Car Parking:
Parking available at Caernarfon
Coach Parking:
At Victoria Docks (¼ mile from Caernarfon station) and in Porthmadog
Souvenir Shop(s): Yes
Food & Drinks:
Full buffet available on most trains

SPECIAL INFO

The Railway has been reconstructed between Caernarfon and Porthmadog Harbour along the track bed of the original Welsh Highland Railway. 2011 saw the completion of this spectacular route passing from coast to coast through the majestic scenery of the Snowdonia National Park.

OPERATING INFO

Opening Times: 2015 dates: Regular services run from 24th March to 1st November. There is also a limited service in the Winter and Santa Specials on weekends in December. Train times vary depending on the date. Please contact the railway for further details.
Steam Working:
Most trains are steam-hauled.
Prices: Adult £35.80 (Round trip return)
Concessions £32.20 (Round trip)
One child travels free with each adult or concessionary fare and additional children travel for half the fare.
Concessionary prices are available for Senior Citizens and groups of 20 or more and cheaper fares are available for single rides and shorter journeys.

Detailed Directions by Car:
Take either the A487(T), the A4085 or the A4086 to Caernarfon then follow the brown tourist signs for the Railway which is situated in St. Helens Road next to the Castle.

WELSHPOOL & LLANFAIR LIGHT RAILWAY

Address: The Station, Llanfair Caereinion, Powys SY21 0SF
Telephone Nº: (01938) 810441
Year Formed: 1959
Location of Line: Welshpool to Llanfair Caereinion, Mid Wales
Length of Line: 8 miles

Nº of Steam Locos: 9
Nº of Other Locos: 5
Nº of Members: 2,200
Annual Membership Fee: £25.00
Approx Nº of Visitors P.A.: 26,000
Gauge: 2 feet 6 inches
Web site: www.wllr.org.uk

GENERAL INFORMATION

Nearest Mainline Station: Welshpool (1 mile)
Nearest Bus Station: Welshpool (1 mile)
Car Parking: Free parking at Welshpool and Llanfair Caereinion
Coach Parking: As above
Souvenir Shop(s): Yes – at both ends of line
Food & Drinks: Yes – at Llanfair only

SPECIAL INFORMATION

The railway has the steepest gradient of any British railway, reaching a summit of 603 feet.

OPERATING INFORMATION

Opening Times: 2015 dates: Every weekend and Bank Holiday from 28th March to 1st November. Daily from 19th May to 27th September. Closed on all Mondays and Fridays in June and September and most Mondays and Fridays in July. Santa Specials operate on 12th, 13th, 19th & 20th December. Trains usually run from around 10.00am until 5.00pm.
Steam Working: All trains are steam-hauled
Prices: Adult Day Rover £12.80
  Senior Citizen Day Rover £11.80
  Under-16s Day Rover £4.00
  (Must be accompanied)
Children under the age of 3 travel free of charge.

Detailed Directions by Car:
Both stations are situated alongside the A458 Shrewsbury to Dolgellau road and are clearly signposted

West Lancashire Light Railway

<table>
<tr><td>

Address: Station Road, Hesketh Bank,
Nr. Preston, Lancashire   PR4 6SP
Telephone Nº: (01772) 815881
Year Formed: 1967
Location of Line: On former site of Alty's
Brickworks, Hesketh Bank
Length of Line: ¼ mile

</td><td>

Nº of Steam Locos: 8
Nº of Other Locos: 24
Nº of Members: Approximately 110
Annual Membership Fee: £15.00 Adult;
£20.00 Family
Approx Nº of Visitors P.A.: 14,500
Gauge: 2 feet
Web site: www.westlancs.org

</td></tr>
</table>

GENERAL INFORMATION

Nearest Mainline Station: Rufford (4 miles)
Nearest Bus Station: Preston (7 miles)
Car Parking: Space for 50 cars at site
Coach Parking: Space for 3 coaches at site
Souvenir Shop(s): Yes
Food & Drinks: Only soft drinks & snacks

SPECIAL INFORMATION

The Railway is run by volunteers and there is a large
collection of Industrial Narrow Gauge equipment.

OPERATING INFORMATION

Opening Times: 2015 dates: Sundays and Bank
Holidays from April to the end of October. Santa
Specials on 12th, 13th, 19th and 20th December and
other Special Events are held during the year.
Trains run from 11.30am to 5.00pm.
Steam Working: Trains operate on Sundays and
Bank Holidays from April until the end of October.
Prices: Adult £2.50   Child £1.50
        Family Tickets £6.00
        Senior Citizens £2.00
Note: Different fares apply for Gala Days and Santa
Specials.

Detailed Directions by Car:
Travel by the A59 from Liverpool or Preston or by the A565 from Southport to the junction of the two roads at
Tarleton. From here follow signs to Hesketh Bank. The Railway is signposted.

WICKSTEED PARK RAILWAY

Address: Wicksteed Park, Kettering, NN15 6NJ	**Nº of Steam Locos:** None
Telephone Nº: (01536) 512475	**Nº of Other Locos:** 3
Year Formed: 1931	**Approx Nº of Visitors P.A.:** 200,000 (visitors to Wicksteed Park)
Location of Line: Wicksteed Park	**Gauge:** 2 feet
Length of Line: 1¼ miles	**Web site:** www.wicksteedpark.co.uk

GENERAL INFORMATION

Nearest Mainline Station: Kettering (2 miles)
Nearest Bus Station: Kettering (2 miles)
Car Parking: Available on site (£6.00 entrance fee per car in the Summer, £4.00 Autumn, £2.00 Spring)
Coach Parking: Free parking available on site
Souvenir Shop(s): Yes
Food & Drinks: Available

SPECIAL INFORMATION

The Railway runs through the grounds of a large leisure complex, Wicksteed Park, which also houses many other attractions including a fairground, a rollercoaster and a log chute ride.

OPERATING INFORMATION

Opening Times: 2015 dates: Open at weekends from 28th March to 1st November, daily during the school holidays and from 27th June to 6th September. Open from 10.30am to 6.00pm in the Summer and until 4.30pm at other times.
Steam Working: None at present.
Prices: As a wide variety of rides are available, sheets of ride tickets can be purchased at a rate of £1.25 each or £33.00 for 40 tickets. Each trip on the railway costs 2 ride tickets. Alternatively wristbands which allow unlimited use of all attractions on the day of purchase are also available priced at £18.00 for Children, £15.00 for Adults and £9.00 for Senior Citizens. Group discounts are also available.

Detailed Directions by Car:
From the North: Exit the M1 at Junction 19 and take the A14 towards Kettering. Leave the A14 at Junction 10 and follow signs for Wicksteed Park. Alternatively take the A1 to Stamford, the A43 to Kettering then the A14 as above; From the South: Exit the M1 at Junction 15 and take the A43 to the junction with the A14, then as above. Alternatively take the A1 to the Junction with the A14 then continue to Junction 10 as above.

WINDMILL ANIMAL FARM RAILWAY

Address: Windmill Animal Farm,
Red Cat Lane, Burscough   L40 1UQ
Telephone Nº: (07971) 221343
Year Formed: 1997
Location of Line: Burscough, Lancashire
Length of Line: 1 mile

Nº of Steam Locos: 5
Nº of Other Locos: 6
Approx Nº of Visitors P.A.: 40,000
Gauge: 15 inches
Web: www.windmillanimalfarm.co.uk

GENERAL INFORMATION

Nearest Mainline Station: Burscough (2½ miles)
Nearest Bus Station: Southport (8½ miles)
Car Parking: Available at the Farm
Coach Parking: Available at the Farm
Souvenir Shop(s): Yes
Food & Drinks: Available

SPECIAL INFORMATION

In addition to the railway, the site includes a play
area and a large number of farm animals with a
petting area where children can feed the animals.

OPERATING INFORMATION

Opening Times: 2015 dates: Open Daily from 28th
March until 1st November and during weekends and
school holidays at all other times. Trains run from
11.00am to 4.30pm.
Steam Working: Every weekend
Prices: Adult Admission £6.00 (Farm entrance)
              Child Admission £7.00 (Farm entrance)
              Senior Citizen Admission £4.50 (Farm ent.)
              Family Admission £24.00 (Farm entrance)
Train Rides: Adult £1.50
                  Child £1.00 (Under-2s ride free)

Detailed Directions by Car:
From All Parts: Exit the M6 at Junction 27 and take the A5209 following signs for Southport. On entering
Burscough follow signs for Burscough Bridge and Martin Lane. Turn left into Red Cat Lane just by Burscough
Bridge train station and follow the road along for Windmill Animal Farm and the Railway.

WOODHORN NARROW GAUGE RAILWAY

Address: Woodhorn Northumberland Museum, Queen Elizabeth II Country Park, Ashington NE63 9YF
Telephone Nº: 0790 600-9569
Year Formed: 1995
Location of Line: Northumberland
Length of Line: 1,000 yards

Nº of Steam Locos: None
Nº of Other Locos: 3
Approx Nº of Visitors P.A.: 100,000 (to the museum); 25,000 (to the railway)
Gauge: 2 feet
Web site: woodhornnarrowgaugerailway.weebly.com

GENERAL INFORMATION

Nearest Mainline Station: Morpeth (8 miles)
Nearest Bus Station: Ashington (1 mile)
Car Parking: Available on site (£3.00 charge)
Coach Parking: Available
Souvenir Shop(s): Yes
Food & Drinks: Available

SPECIAL INFORMATION

The railway runs through the grounds of the Woodhorn Museum and is operated by volunteers. Wheelchair access is available on trains by request.

OPERATING INFORMATION

Opening Times: Weekends and Bank Holidays throughout the year and daily during School Holidays, weather permitting. Open from 10.00am to 5.00pm (4.00pm during the winter months). The last train departs at 3.30pm (at 2.30pm during the winter).
Steam Working: None
Prices: Adults £2.00
　　　　 Children £1.00

Detailed Directions by Car:
From All Parts: Take the A1 to the A19 at Cramlington then the A189 towards Ashington and follow the brown tourist signs for Woodhorn. (Beware of SatNav directions which may leave you on the wrong side of the local goods railway line!)
